What We Talk About When We Talk
About Love: *Bookmarked*

The *Bookmarked* Series

Raymond Carver's

What We Talk About When We Talk About Love:

BOOKMARKED

BRIAN EVENSON

Kirby Gann, *Series Editor*

PUBLISHING

Ig Publishing
Box 2547
New York, NY 10163
www.igpub.com

I have tried to recreate events, locales and conversations as accurately as possible from my memory of them, supported by contemporaneous documents, materials, notes, and other sources. Names and identifying details have very occasionally been omitted to protect the privacy of individuals.

ISBN: 978-1-63246-070-7

PRINTED IN THE UNITED STATES OF AMERICA
FIRST EDITION

Raymond Carver's

What We Talk About When We Talk About Love:

BOOKMARKED

Prologue

ON THE EVENING OF JULY 4TH OF 2011, I STARTED VOMITING and found it impossible to stop. I was just back from two weeks of teaching a fiction writing workshop in Portugal, where I'd felt a little worse each day. At first, I thought I was just tired because of the time difference between Rhode Island and Europe, then that I had a cold, then that maybe it was flu. I slept more and more, felt increasingly disoriented. I was having trouble breathing, but I told myself this was just an indication that I was out of shape, that the more I walked the better I'd feel. On the back of my story collection *Windeye* there's a picture of me standing in the palace of Sintra where if you look closely you'll see my eyes are glassy, my face filmed with sweat. I'm smiling, but desperately so. I was trying to act like I was fine. I was, after all, the teacher. I was there to be the one who helped others, not the one who needed help.

By the time I was convinced I needed a doctor, the workshop was almost over. Since I found daunting the idea of going to a doctor in a country where I didn't speak the language, I opted to stick it out and wait until I got home.

But standing in the Lisbon airport early in the afternoon of Saturday July 2nd, I realized that things were much worse than I had supposed. I couldn't stop sweating, I had no appetite, I felt increasingly disoriented, and I was suffering from paracusia, beginning to experience auditory hallucinations. The last time I'd had paracusia had been three or four years earlier when I'd had the flu and had driven with my then-girlfriend from Oklahoma to Rhode Island without adequate sleep, desperate to make it home to my own bed. Maybe it was flu after all, I thought, and then hoped the worst of the symptoms wouldn't strike until I'd landed.

The Sata airlines flight home seems to me now more of a hallucination than an actuality, in that disconnected and partial way that you (or at least I) remember things when you're very drunk indeed, as scattered bits and pieces with a kind of absence where you yourself normally reside—a few moments you can cling to, a great deal that's just lost and may come back later or not at all. I had not been drinking. I had had nothing to drink except water, and very little of that, and nothing to eat for some hours. It seemed a very long flight to me, and I have no memory of the three hour and forty minute stop we took in the Azores, at Ponta Delgada, despite some of the workshop participants on the same flight telling me later that I'd participated coherently in several conversations, that they'd had little sense that something was wrong with me.

I do remember landing in Boston, exhausted, and my then-girlfriend picking me up and then the two of us driving home. I don't remember if she drove or I did—I suspect the latter since I almost always did the driving, but I can't be sure. I believe I told her that I'd been feeling poorly, but, as I often did (and still sometimes do), downplayed how ill I actually was.

Once home, I collapsed. Perhaps a night at home in my own bed would be enough to revive me. I slept deeply for a few hours, then restlessly, then not at all. I had a pain in my right side, just below my rib cage, and was having trouble breathing. When I stood, I felt dizzy. I wandered the house delirious as my then-girlfriend slept.

And yet, now that I was back home, despite my experience on the plane, despite what I was feeling, I tried to tell myself it was nothing to worry about. It was as if I could stop myself from being ill just by force of will, by convincing myself I *wasn't* ill. When I had been a Mormon missionary decades before, I'd bought a punk cassette which I no longer have and the name of which I no longer remember at a flea market in Marseilles (we were forbidden to listen to anything but hymns as missionaries but that rule, like so many others, I didn't keep). It included a sung parody of a "diagnostic rite for health," with someone screaming "I have been ill, I must get better!" over and over again. Early on the morning of July 3rd, I was thinking about this song, repeating it obsessively over and over again in my head as I waited for the sun to rise.

It was Sunday. I did not feel human. The paracusia had returned and it felt like several people were standing just outside of my field of vision, mumbling something that, I began to feel, was about me. Every once in a while, a voice would rise up out of the mumbling, its tones clearer and pitch higher but still not legible. I could recognize it as an individual voice, but could not recognize what it was saying. *You're going mad*, I told myself, but another part of me knew I was not going mad, that I was ill, that I had experienced this before, and that once I was better, the paracusia would end.

It was that as much as anything that got me to the doctor—an eagerness to end the auditory hallucinations. I walked down the hill to the end of our street and went right a half block to the clinic located there and then, since I hadn't realized the clinic opened an hour later on Sundays, and couldn't face the thought of having to walk back up the hill only to walk down again in an hour, found a place to sit and wait until it did open. When it did, I went in, signed in, waited, signed various forms, waited some more, met with a physician's assistant, explained what was happening, had x-rays taken, had my blood drawn. I had a fever. There was nothing to be seen on the x-rays. The PA suggested I go home to rest and drink lots of fluids. He told me they'd call the next day with the results of the blood tests.

"Or, well," he said, "not tomorrow, since tomorrow is Fourth of July. We'll have results back from the lab on Tuesday."

Okay, I said, and stumbled home. I tried to sleep. My head felt very hot. The voices were still there. I felt vaguely nauseous and couldn't stop sweating. I was hardly coherent, but I could fake coherency for brief moments. *Maybe I'll feel better tomorrow*, I told myself.

My then-girlfriend had been invited to a Fourth of July party, I no longer remember where, with people who were more her friends than mine. I was invited as well, but I didn't feel up to going. But was it okay if she went? she wanted to know. I didn't see much point in her staying, and she clearly was eager to go, so I said yes, even encouraged her.

An hour later, I started vomiting. On one level I felt as sick as I've ever felt. On another level, I was so sick, so incoherent, so receded from the surface of my body, that it was as if this was happening to someone else. I did not call my girlfriend, though in retrospect it seems that would have been the best thing to do. At least I don't think I called her—if I did, she didn't answer. Instead, I lay there, in the bathroom, vomiting, shivering, with a soaring fever. Sometimes I would manage to make it back to the bed for a few minutes, sometimes not. When she came home, I told her I needed to go to the emergency room—or maybe she was the one to make that decision. My memory of it, the way I tell the story to myself now that we are broken up and haven't spoken in several years, is that it was the first thing I said to her when she walked through the door.

At the emergency room, things sped up in some ways,

slowed down in others. If you are not in danger of bleeding out or flatlining, a good part of your time in an emergency room involves waiting in a curtained-off semi-room as things happen around you. The pain in my side was fairly intense now. I was given some sort of painkiller, I no longer remember what. I was given an ultrasound, but at some point was taken away for a CT scan as well. My heart was now beating much faster than it normally did, laboring, and it would not slow down.

I had, I would eventually be told, a serious infection that had led to a collapsed lung. I had had my appendix out at the same hospital eight months earlier and the doctor's best guess was that a small fragment of infected appendiceal tissue had not been removed from my body. It had floated through my tissues for months before finally attaching to the top of my liver where it had formed an abscess, which had led to a fistula forming in my thoracic cavity and the cavity filling with fluid, which in turn had collapsed the lung.

Early Tuesday morning they sent me off to have the fluid drained. A man with a thick Rhode Island accent and what, because of some cartoon I watched as a kid, I think of as a sanitation worker's mustache, pushed a needle deep into my back. The needle was connected by a tube to a large jar which rapidly began filling with pus-like fluid. He filled two jars.

I felt better momentarily, until abruptly I didn't again. Soon I had trouble breathing. By 10:00 AM Tuesday morning, they determined that the cavity had filled with fluid again. They sent me off to have an CT scan so that they could better determine what was happening and how to treat it, telling my then-girlfriend I would be away for fifteen or twenty minutes.

My last memory was of lying on a board as a nurse and a technician tried to position me for the scan. A board? Could I really have been on a board? I started shaking and couldn't stop. And then I became unresponsive and blacked out.

I woke up surrounded by the concerned faces of half a dozen nurses. I was not in the room I had been in, and did not know how I had gotten to where I was. "There you are," one of them said, which struck me as a strange thing to say. As I began to come conscious and proved myself capable of responding to questions, several of the nurses visibly relaxed. Soon, all but two of them had moved off to other tasks.

Four hours had passed.

Eventually, I was wheeled back to my room. I had to, or rather felt I had to, calm down my distraught girlfriend, who had been told little during my absence, and so I downplayed what had happened. That had, generally, been my role in the relationship—to be the calm one—and I had learned the role well enough to do it almost by rote, even when I was heavily drugged and it was absurd.

I had only been back in the room a few minutes when my cell phone rang. In an effort to prove that I was perfectly fine, that I had not just almost died, I took the call. It was the PA from the clinic.

"Mr. Evenson?" he said.

"Yes?" I said.

"I have the results of your blood test," he said. "You have a serious infection. You need to go to the hospital immediately."

"I'm already at the hospital," I said.

"Good," he said. "Thank God."

I wasn't sure how to respond to this. When he didn't continue, I didn't know what else to do but hang up.

A day or two later, a doctor with no bedside manner would make an incision in my side, drive a hard plastic spike through my ribs, and then thread a tube in, connecting it to a machine that would actively draw the fluid from me. When the spike went in, the fluid rushed out and soaked the doctor's shoes, and my lung suddenly inflated. It was the single most painful thing I've ever experienced, and the remainder of my time in the hospital I spent dreading that they would have to drive another spike in. Months later, I was still having nightmares about it.

I was in the hospital for two weeks in all, during which time I lost 22 percent of my body weight. During the first week, I was sick enough and sufficiently sedated to not be focused on what was going on around me. I could not walk to the end of the hall and back without needing to rest. In the second week, though, I gradually became aware that something else was wrong. My girlfriend seemed to be acting strangely. She struck me as reluctant to be there, fidgeted, seemed eager to be gone. Thinking back, I realized she had been like this even before, on the night she went off on her own to the Fourth of July party, probably even before I left for Portugal. When I finally left the hospital on July 18th, I would discover that she had started searching for an apartment and was planning to move out. We tried to patch things back together, but a few weeks later we would break up for good.

All of that contributed to my frame of mind: the most serious illness of my life to date, an impending breakup, a sense of physical frailty, an inability to focus mentally. My girlfriend came to pick me up at the hospital and then seemed angry that they hadn't released me by the time she arrived. We only lived a few blocks away from the hospital and I remember—I think this is an accurate memory and not instead a memory from when I had my appendix removed (the two illnesses are linked in my mind since one caused the other)—walking back to the house exceptionally slowly, stopping three or four times each block to catch my breath. But perhaps I only walked to the car.[1]

Once home, I moved slowly, like an old man, to our hallway, and regarded myself in the full-length mirror. I had

---

1. "[N]ot only have I always had trouble distinguishing between what happened and what merely might have happened, but I remain unconvinced that the distinction, for my purposes, matters." Joan Didion, "On Keeping a Notebook," in *Slouching Towards Bethlehem* (New York: FSG, 1968), 134.

looked at myself in the mirror in the hospital sometimes, but here, at home, looking into a mirror I had looked into often, I could not help but see how much I had changed. So much so that I had difficulty recognizing myself.

•

Looking at myself in the mirror, I found myself thinking of Raymond Carver's "The Father," from his 1976 story collection, *Will You Please Be Quiet, Please*? I hadn't read that story in probably two decades. And yet, looking over it just a few months ago as I began to work on this book, I discovered that despite the time that had passed, I remembered it almost perfectly.

It's a short piece, just two pages, more of an anecdote than a story. In it, a family sits around a new baby, engaged in the familiar ritual of attributing parts of the baby to the family member they most resemble. But each time one of them says the baby has someone's toes, or lips or eyes, the others remain unsatisfied, feeling what has been said isn't quite right. Until the baby's sister says, "I know! I know! He looks like Daddy!"

"But who does Daddy look like?" asks another sister. She answers herself a little later, beginning to cry, "Why, nobody!"

And indeed, a moment later, in the unnerving single sentence paragraph that ends the story, we have the father described. "He had turned around in his chair and his face was white and without expression."

That was what my face struck me as, white and without expression, as if my sense of self had been stripped away, as if I were more the matrix for a being than a being itself, as if I were no longer part of the human race.

.

I've thought about "The Father" a lot since then. I first encountered that story when Leslie Norris, the Welsh poet who was my mentor, read it aloud to our class because of a story I had written. Rereading "The Father" thirty years later, I still hear the rich cadences of Leslie's voice despite the fact that he has been dead for more than a decade. I realized in late 2013, when I was assembling the collection that would become *A Collapse of Horses*, that I'd had the story in the back of my mind when I wrote "Three Indignities," despite it being a very different sort of story, about a moment of almost unbearable panic during a medical procedure—one of my few autobiographical stories.

What I admire so much about Carver, particularly in his early collections *Will You Please Be Quiet, Please* and *What We Talk About When We Talk About Love*, is his ability to move so rapidly and seamlessly from the ordinary to the uncanny, from the banal to the destructive or debilitative, and to do it with just a few careful strokes. In "The Father" there's a deliberate shifting of terms: it starts as an ordinarily realistic story, presenting a ritual we've all participated in, and only begins to trouble our sense of its realism three-quarters of the way through, waiting to assert itself as a fantastical story or parable until the final line. So you think you're reading one thing and only discover at the end, from the strange, blank presence of the father in the room, that you've been reading quite another.

·

This experience was not unique for me. Indeed, Carver's work has spoken directly to me at some extraordinary moments and in extraordinary ways. He writes about a peculiar and particularly American form of abjection which, even if I never shared the specifics of it (I never really learned how to smoke and though I now drink I can put it down or pick it up with little effort), I still relate to in other ways. In addition, there's a great deal that is unexpected about his work if you look closely at it, particularly if you're a writer. This, as has become clear in recent years, is only partly due to Carver. It is due as well to Gordon Lish, who severely edited his first two books.

I'm not a realist, or rather I don't care if my work is or isn't—I've made a literary career out of muddying that distinction. That, too, is something that I learned from Carver, even though many of his critics, particularly those who favor his later stories, minimize this aspect of his work. But without this, Carver is a great deal less interesting.

Carver's work arrived for me at exactly the right moment. My relationship to that work has changed over time, but of all the writers I read when I was first developing as a writer he, more than anyone except perhaps J. G. Ballard, taught me how to write the fiction that I wanted to write.

One

A LOT OF BOOKS THAT HAD A HUGE FORMATIVE EFFECT on friends or writers I admire I either read at the wrong moment or didn't read at all. Despite spending a decade of summers teaching in Naropa University's Jack Kerouac school, I didn't read *On the Road* until I was nearly forty—and only read it then because it had begun to feel too awkward to confess to pro-Beat students that I hadn't. I read *Catcher in the Rye* in college and enjoyed it, but kept wishing that I'd read it when I'd been in high school, when it might have mattered to me. Vonnegut I only read when I was in my late forties, mainly because I had a free Kindle copy of *Slaughterhouse–Five* that I could read on my phone while I fed my infant son a bottle—it was much easier to swipe and turn a page than try to turn a real page with a baby in my arms—and then went on to read most of the rest of his work. *Under the Volcano*, which I loved when I finally got to it, I read only a few months ago. Other books I did read, but they left me cold.

But two writers stood out for me. I was fourteen and reading pretty much exclusively science fiction and fantasy when my father gave me a copy of *The Basic Kafka.* He sat down and read aloud to me a story he liked: "A Fratricide." It's a minor story, not one of Kafka's best, but there's something about the theatricality of it, the way that people seem to be acting out their roles as much as actually living them, that baffled me in a productive way. It made me realize that imitating life wasn't always the point to fiction. In addition, the novelty of the situation interested me: my mother and father were avid readers, but recommending a book to me so strongly wasn't something my father was prone to do back then, though he often has since. Looking back on it now, I see that as the first moment my father consciously acknowledged me as an adult.

I still love "A Fratricide." I can spend an entire class period talking about it and still have a great deal left to say. But the real Kafka revelation for me was not that nor the much better known "The Metamorphosis," but "A Country Doctor" and "In the Penal Colony." The first did things with replicated doubles that fascinated me and suggested that fiction not only had its own reality separate from imitating life, but that it could strobe between the realistic and a sort of symbolic game. The second introduced me to a notion of language as something that could be inflicted upon someone, and raised questions about the relationship of the state, the individual body, and language. That's not how I would have described it at fourteen, but it's still an accurate representation of what I felt.

The other writer was Samuel Beckett, discovered a year or two later. We had read in our AP English class Edward Albee's *The Zoo Story*. Everybody who read it in our predominantly Mormon and conservative high school seemed to hate the play, except for me and my friend David Beus, who loved it. The note heading the play in our anthology mentioned Beckett's work, though I no longer remember why—perhaps because the first production of *The Zoo Story* was a double bill with *Krapp's Last Tape*. I moved quickly through Beckett's plays, settling on *Endgame* as my favorite, but it wasn't until I read *Molloy* that I realized I had found a writer I would read and reread. I thought of Beckett as writing what I tended to call (perhaps because I had heard someone else say it—I no longer know where the phrase comes from, my head or outside of it) fractured allegories: work with the weight and structure of allegory or symbol but essentially indecipherable. Like Kafka, Beckett showed me you could write something literary whose thrust was narrative but which was not, in any sense, realism.

So, when I got to Carver, I had Beckett and Kafka as models for what I hoped literature could do. Which probably made me see Carver in a very eccentric light.

•

My first encounter with Carver's work was not *What We Talk About When We Talk About Love*, but a story from *Will You Please Be Quiet, Please?* I was eighteen. I had taken Beginning Creative Writing and Intermediate Fiction Writing the first and second semester of my freshman year at Mormon-run Brigham Young University. I'd decided to enroll in the non-required Spring term (half the length of the normal semester) and to take the final undergrad class in the sequence, Advanced Fiction Writing, as well. Since there was no graduate workshop offered for Spring term, the class turned out to consist of a mix of upper classmen and grad students. I was the only freshman in the class. It never crossed my mind that a freshman shouldn't take Advanced Fiction. I don't know what the teacher, Eloise Bell, thought, but for some reason she let me in.

Eloise Bell was at once funny and caustic, exceptionally quick, theatrical—one of the few Mormons I've met with such qualities. The room we met in was unbearably hot. Some of my most vivid memories of the class are all of us sitting in a circle watching one another sweat. Bell, among the most corpulent of us, was a very able perspirer, which to my mind gave her a certain undeniable authority.

It was perhaps the third or fourth class session, early in the term in any case. I arrived a few minutes late to find class just starting. We were sitting, as usual, in a circle, though for some reason the circle was oriented differently than it habitually was, crowded on the side of the classroom with the door on it rather than on the side close to the window where we'd have at least the hint of a breeze. Bell generally sat with her back to the window, nearly touching the wall just below it. Now she sat closest to the door, almost backed against it. Coming into the classroom I had to sidle past her. It felt like she was guarding the door, either keeping people from entering or keeping people from leaving.

I was just taking my seat directly across from her (the only seat left) when she announced that we were going to start by listening to a tape recording of a writer reading his work. Raymond Carver, she said his name was, and I could tell by the appreciative nods that some of the grad students gave that they knew who he was. I had never heard the name. She pressed play and we began to listen, all of us—or me at least—trying to look attentive and thoughtful, staring through each other instead of catching one another's gaze.

The story was "Nobody Said Anything." It's told from the perspective of a boy who wakes up to hear his parents fighting, then fakes illness so he can stay home from school, steals cigarettes (which he calls "weeds") from his mother's purse, beats off, explores his parent's drawers, speculates on how Vaseline might be used for sex, and then leaves the house to go fishing. On the way, he's picked up by an older woman who he fantasizes fucking, though it's clear from the way he imagines it ("She asks me if she can keep her sweater on and I say it's okay with me. She keeps her pants on too. That's all right, I say. I don't mind.") that he has little idea what that might actually entail. The boy's thoughts often stray to sex. He has frequent boners, "shoots off" over a stream, talks about swearing on a bible to stop masturbating but getting jism on the bible in the process. He's very consciously not thinking about his parents' fight, though it continues to wait there, just beneath the surface of his consciousness.

But when he's fishing, when a trout strikes or when he's trying with another boy to catch a long but oddly thin fish, he does almost seem to forget. Pure delight seeps in. Carver's details of that process—descriptions of hooking salmon eggs or affixing the sinkers to the line by biting them—are simple and stripped down, but have great authority. They reminded me vividly of fishing with my father.

In the end, he and the other boy manage to catch the oddly thin fish. They're incredibly proud, but have a hard time knowing how to share the spoils—the glory of the fish is its sheer length, but if one of them takes it home, the other will go home empty-handed. The narrator manages to convince the other boy, shivering because of a fall into the water, to cut the fish in half, then strikes a deal so he can take the half home with the head on it. Excited, he hurries back home, only to find his parents home already and vehemently arguing. When he tries to present his catch, partly as a way of distracting his parents, getting them to share in his joy, they turn on him. "Take that goddam thing out of here!" his father says. "What in the hell is the matter with you? Take it the hell out of the kitchen and throw it in the goddam garbage!" The story ends with the boy outside and alone near the trash can, holding his half fish, not quite willing to let go of the magic of it.

•

What Bell played must have been from the American Audio Prose Library's 1983 recording of three Carver stories—"Nobody Said Anything," "A Serious Talk," and "Fat." Would "Fat" or "A Serious Talk" have had as much impact on me if either had been my first Carver story? I don't think so. The characters in "A Serious Talk," when I did read it, reminded me of older versions of friends I had, people I worked with at Hamburger World, the local burger joint where I'd been employed throughout high school, or the older brothers and sisters of kids I'd gone to school with. But I was insulated from that life: I knew I wasn't those people. "Fat" might have—the viscerality of that story, a fat man eating and the dislocation between the waitress's sense of him and everybody else's view of him, the way she feels at once driven to talk about him and unable to express herself in a way that captures what the experience was for her listener, were different from anything I'd read before. And the story offered a painful insight into the complexity of sexuality that, idealistic and eighteen, I probably was far from ready for. It was a story I thought about often once I did read it. But even that, because it had a female central character who was quite different from me, felt safer to me.

But was that just because it was the second Carver story I read, not the first? That I'd already begun to understand what to expect?

What hurt me about "Nobody Said Anything" was the thought that I might be more like this masturbating kid, coyly called only "R.", than I wanted to believe. Joan Didion speaks in *My Year of Magical Thinking* of how "People who have recently lost someone have a certain look, recognizable maybe only to those who have seen that look on their own faces ... The look is one of extreme vulnerability, nakedness, openness."[2] That was something the story expressed to me: the boy, despite his bluster, managed over the course of his narrative to lay himself bare, recounting for the first time his consciousness of the collapse of his parents' relationship and a trauma that he would continue to have to recount for years to come. It struck me that Carver was giving voice not only to his character's trauma but to a trauma of his own, and calling upon me, uncomfortably, to share it because of all the ways that I was like this kid. It was a story that did a great deal more work for me after it was finished than it did on the page: it was a story that would continue to evolve and change as I thought about it. Until I read "Nobody Said Anything," I didn't know a story could do that.

I remember Carver reading the story flatly—nonchalantly and almost crudely, it seemed to me—which made

2. Joan Didion, *The Year of Magical Thinking* (New York: Alfred A. Knopf, 2005), 74–75.

the story's impact all the greater. I suspect that Bell chose to have us listen to that story just because it was the first one on the tape. If not, perhaps it was because it was the longest story and we hadn't yet reached the point in the class of workshopping so there was ample time to fill. As we all listened to it, facing one another, my façade began to break. Soon I was darting glances at others, but people were still going to great pains not to react and to look serious. The story upset me, and I had a hard time not revealing that it had. I did not want people to know how deeply it had spoken to me, because that would reveal, I feared, too much about me.

Once the story ended, Bell clicked off the recorder. She swept us with her gaze, and then said, "Thoughts?" When nobody volunteered, she began to go around the circle, asking us one by one what we thought of the story.

I don't remember specifically what anybody said, but I do remember growing more and more agitated, partly because my turn was coming, and partly because the measured responses that the more advanced students were giving seemed to me to have very little to do with what the story was or what it was trying to do—what, anyway, it had done to me. I felt dully angry, but resentful too that I would soon have to speak.

When my turn came, I don't remember what I said either. Something offhand and semi-sarcastic, just a sentence or two, a vague lashing out partly at Carver's story for ambushing me, partly at the other students for not having a more visceral response. I was young and fairly naïve, and probably a bit of an asshole. Looking back at the story now, just having reread it, I have a hard time seeing why it shocked me so much. But it still strikes me as a great story, and a painfully honest one.

I remember Bell listening and then asking if I could clarify what I meant. I struggled, offered something equally vague, tried again, failed, and then shrugged, hoping perhaps she'd be able to give me a way to phrase what I'd failed to express. Instead, she simply looked at me for a moment without expression and then moved on to the student sitting beside me.

As it would turn out, this was for me the best possible response.

•

I was looking for a box to put the story in. It had made me uncomfortable, and if I'd had an easy way to dismiss it, I would have. I was groping for that in the few words I was forced to say after just having listened to it. But my response was complex in that I was objecting to the other students' approach for that very reason—they had ready-made boxes they could put the story in, but they didn't strike me as boxes that could actually, if properly considered, contain the story.

If I'd read the story on the page, rather than hearing someone say "beat off" and "goddamn" aloud, I would have been able to metabolize it easier. One of the shocking things about the story, in retrospect, was that I first heard it on BYU's campus. Mormons were not supposed to take the name of God in vain, and that was particularly true of BYU students. Indeed, we had a strict code of conduct that concerned not only the language we were allowed to use but every aspect of our lives. To attend BYU you had to remain worthy members of the Mormon church and have your worthiness periodically affirmed by your ecclesiastical leaders. You could not drink alcohol, drink coffee, or smoke. You could not have sex (or, well, you could as long as both you and the person you were having sex with kept it a secret). Boys were supposed to report if they masturbated to their Bishop and had to strive to stop, and could in fact be suspended from the university if the practice continued. You were not allowed to take the name of the Lord in vain—if I'd said the word "goddamn" in front of the wrong person (I said this and more, of course, but always with great awareness of who was in earshot) I would have been reported for a conduct violation.

In addition, you had to live in BYU-approved housing. The dormitories, where I lived as a freshman, were strictly divided by gender. You were not allowed to visit the room of someone from the opposite gender except for a few hours on Sunday, when visits were strictly monitored and doors always left wide open. If you snuck into the room of someone of the opposite gender at another time, you could be suspended.

There was more. Men's hair had to be cut short, off the back of their collar with the ears not covered by hair. If you violated this, or had what was judged an extreme hairstyle, you could get reported. There was a strict dress code you would get reported for violating as well—no tank tops for either men or women, no shirts that would reveal the belly, and all shorts had to fall at least to the middle of the knee. This had to do with the particulars of the Mormon garment, the sacred underwear that Mormons who had been on a mission wore underneath their clothing.

Mormonism is a strangely bifurcated religion. On the surface, it seems largely protestant: a secular ministry with weekly church services at a local meeting house that are open to anyone. But there's a second, ritualized layer to Mormonism, consisting of what goes on in the Mormon temple. In 1984–85, when I was a freshman at BYU, this involved a sacred (and consequently secret) Masonic-style passion play made up of watching movies, putting on and rearranging ritual clothing, engaging in promises and handshakes, and exchanging ritual phrases. You made promises not to reveal the secrets, and then mimed how you would kill yourself if you did.[3] To participate in the Mormon temple ceremonies, you have to receive your "temple endowment," a particular ceremony where you are first introduced to the mysteries of the temple and are

3. This portion of the Mormon temple ceremony, the "penalties" phase, was dropped a few years later.

given a new name that you are told you must keep secret.[4] To receive your endowment, you have to be a member in exceptionally good standing, and I'd guess well over half the people on the active rolls of the Mormon church have never gone, so it's as if there's a secret society hidden within the Mormon church.

In 1985, as a freshman, I hadn't been endowed yet—I would be endowed a year or so later as I prepared to go on a Mormon mission to Switzerland. But I'd been raised Mormon all my life. I knew there were disjunctions between how Mormons acted in private and public. I wasn't averse to swearing or privately violating boundaries that I publicly seemed to affirm. But despite that, I was stunned to see it being done in class at a Mormon-controlled university. One part of me felt it was deeply inappropriate. Another part of me was simply amazed and eager for more.

•

Looking back, I can't help but be impressed by the risk Professor Bell took. If any student had chosen to report the story as "inappropriate"—code for a range of things objectionable to Mormon culture—she would have had a lot to answer for. At the very least, she would have had her hands slapped. When I returned to teach at BYU almost a decade

---

4. I've described some of this in more detail in the middle of my novel *The Open Curtain*, feeling that now that I'm an excommunicated Mormon the promise of secrecy no longer applies.

later, I discovered that there was a committee that quietly looked over the books you assigned to your class. If one of your books had been the subject of past controversy or complaint, the committee chair would "helpfully" call you and let you know. If a book you were planning to teach was unfamiliar to the committee, the chair would call— as, indeed, he did with me—and ask you to "vouch for it." "We're not telling you you can't teach it," I was told about one of the books I was teaching, "that would be censorship." But my guess is that that feeling of being monitored alone was enough to encourage most BYU professors to self-censor.

•

Unsettled by "Nobody Said Anything," I felt I had two choices: either to reject the story wholesale or to scrutinize it and try to crack the code of how it did what it did to me. I don't know why I chose to opt for the latter. Perhaps it was partly because I was ashamed of not having been able to articulate a response to the story. Perhaps it went back to something I remembered Mormon prophet Brigham Young saying: "I mean to learn all that is in heaven, earth, and hell."[5] I wanted to know more than I wanted to be comfortable. Or perhaps it was just sheer cussedness.

5. Brigham Young, *Journal of Discourses*, Vol. 2 (Liverpool: F.D. Richards, 1855). Discourse 2, page 94.

In any case, after class I went to check the book that contained "Nobody Said Anything" out of the BYU library. There was only one copy and it was already checked out. So I went to the bookstore and bought it, and then, instead of studying for the following day's classes, read it straight through. On the page, "Nobody Said Anything" felt more poignant and painful than shocking, but there were other stories that had a similar effect for me. "Fat," the second story I ever read by Carver, struck me nearly as hard, and "Neighbors" had a kind of oddness to it that appealed to me very much—not the same emotional impact, but there was something damaged about it that was nonetheless profoundly human. "They're Not Your Husband" reminded me of how one of my high school friends used to act when he was drunk and had lost all of his filters. "Why, Honey?"—a story about a politician with a vicious hidden past, told by his mother after she's been tracked down by a reporter, worked away at me long after I had finished it. Critic Adam Meyer rightly calls it "one of the most technically dazzling stories in the collection."[6] Indeed, all of the stories, even the ones I didn't like as well, struck me as different from anything else I'd read.

And so, as soon as I'd finished, still hungry for more, I went back to the bookstore. I managed to get there just a few moments before it closed. They had two other Carver books in paperback: *What We Talk About When We Talk*

6. Adam Meyer, *Raymond Carver* (New York: Twayne, 1995), 58.

About Love and the newer paperback, *Cathedral.* Because the repetition in the title of *What We Talk About When We Talk About Love* reminded me of the repeated "Please" in *Will You Please Be Quiet, Please?* and because the book was two dollars cheaper than *Cathedral,* I bought that one.

Two

It's funny to think of those moments when a path forks, when you make a choice, without knowing it at the time, that ends up having a profound impact on your writing or your life. And to think, too, of the missed chances, the moments when we made a wrong choice and perhaps will never know what could have happened, what we missed. A good many of Carver's stories involve characters who seem to have been so drunk that they didn't even know they were on a path to begin with, let alone that the path had forked. Or maybe they drink because they sense those missed moments, those old wounds, rising to the surface again, and want to try to push them back down.

·

Later, teaching at BYU and after some controversy over my first book, *Altmann's Tongue*, I was told by administrators there that if I wanted to stay on as a faculty member

I needed to understand that publishing *Altmann's Tongue* was wrong and that further publications like it would bring "repercussions." In other words, I would be allowed to stay a faculty member as long as I agreed not to publish. I chose to leave and take a one-year position at Oklahoma State University—not an easy decision, since at the time I had two young daughters and a wife to support. A few years later, still being subtly pressured by church leaders about my fiction, I made the decision to leave Mormonism and asked to be formally excommunicated. My then-wife, Connie, remained Mormon. We drifted further and further apart, and eventually divorced. As I was waiting for my official letter from the church telling me that, as they arcanely phrased it, my name had been "blotted from the records of the church," I found myself worrying obsessively that I would go to hell. But as soon as the official letter arrived stripping me of salvation, I felt nothing but immense relief and freedom.

When my girlfriend and I broke up after my near-death in the hospital, I felt an immense despair. For weeks, I kept the same CD in the car stereo and listened to it over and over again, feeling, I suppose, that it was the only stable thing in my life. We have these moments where we feel like we've been torn out of life in some manner, and it's difficult, almost impossible even, to imagine how we will ever be brought back in. Even if we've been there before, have had our suffering eventually mitigated before, each dislocation is painful and new. What Didion talks about in the faces of people who have recently lost someone, that look of "extreme vulnerability, nakedness, openness" manifests in a lesser way, I think, for those smaller losses—divorce or breaking up, illness, loss of religion or job.

And yet most of us do manage to move on. We manage to piece ourselves back together, make a new life for ourselves, eventually begin to feel like we are resident in the world again. And, if we're lucky, whatever the losses of the past, however unimaginable the future, we learn to live more fully in the present world than with the ghosts and regrets of the past.

Now, six years after my hospital stay, I'm married to the writer Kristen Tracy, a woman I deeply love, and we have a four-year-old child. That previous relationship had become more of a holding pattern than a relationship: I was fairly comfortably (or at least not unbearably) stuck, but stuck nonetheless. It wasn't until illness cut the ground out from under me that I was able to shake my way free of that relationship and find the life and partner I both needed and wanted. If I look back on that other life, it's with melancholy, but also with a sense of it being fully over, being past, almost as if it happened to someone else. And yet, if I hadn't had that illness, inertia would have probably kept me in the eddies of that other relationship, and I would have been satisfied with *good enough* rather than *good*.

There's really only one story in *What We Talk About When We Talk About Love* that strikes me as being narrated fully from that vantage, with someone looking back on their past from a point of melancholic stability: "Everything Stuck to Him."[7] It is also the only story in the volume set outside of the United States (it takes place in Italy)—indeed, one of only a few stories in the volume set outside of the Pacific Northwest. About a fight followed by a moment of love and closeness, it's my least favorite story in the volume. But having it there among the other stories of blunt difficulty and drunken struggle does give the sense that yes, these things can be lived through, these things can, no matter how bad they seem at the time, be survived.

•

Back when I was still Mormon, still married to a Mormon and living in Seattle, I was a counselor in a bishopric, one of three people directing a congregation of several hundred people. I've talked elsewhere[8] about one of my jobs sometimes being to go out and meet people who had ended up in Seattle without resources, people in distress, often late at night: people at the end of their rope financially, people who had no place to stay, people who couldn't afford shelter or food. I'd talk with them, sometimes use church funds to buy them a meal or groceries, help them find a job, try to make things possible for them. Most of them were stuck, though also a little baffled about what had happened to

7. Carver's original title for the story, "Distance," perhaps reveals a little too well what the story is intended to convey.
8. Cf. the afterword for the paperback version of *Altmann's Tongue*.

them. Most of them didn't get unstuck because of our help. Or they might get free of their difficulties momentarily and then slip back again.

Most of the characters in *What We Talk About . . .* are like that: numb, wounded, and unable to break free of the trap that they've had a hand in creating. But they keep struggling, keep trying. Or try at least to sort through the past again, set up the chess pieces again and see if the game plays out any differently, try—and fail—to understand where exactly they went wrong. Or even if they do understand, be incapable of making things different.

•

There are the complex paths that fork in life, but for writers there are paths that fork with books. Sometimes a simple, almost random choice opens a field of possibilities. For instance, on a whim I pick up a book called *Berg* in a used bookstore on Tottenham Court Road, largely because I like the cover. It's by an author I've never heard of, Ann Quin, and begins, "A man called Berg, who changed his name to Greb, came to a seaside town intending to kill his father . . ." The book does something with overlapping different levels of discourse that I've never seen before, and leads me as a writer to figure out how to do things that I've never done before. A year later I've read everything by Quin, and then I co-write an article about her, and then I'm asked to write the introduction to the reissue of one of her books, and then, when I take a job at Brown University, I'm hired at the same time as poet Robert Creeley, and we strike up a friendship over the fact that he was a close friend of Quin's.

In the BYU bookstore back in 1985, I know I'm going to buy another Raymond Carver book, and I'm holding both *What We Talk About* and *Cathedral*.

If I'd bought *Cathedral* I would have thought, as I thought later, Hmmm. Solid collection, some decent stories, but very little surprising about it. The stories are fuller, longer, with more interior space. They are well written but, at least to my ear, do not stand out as distinct from other well-written stories I've read. *Cathedral* has few of the gestures and qualities that I admired in *Will You Please Be Quiet, Please?* I remember just a few of the stories. I remember "Cathedral" largely because I've taught it in conjunction with D. H. Lawrence's "The Blind Man," which it is a fairly direct response to. I remember "A Small, Good Thing" because I've taught it in relationship to its other version in *What We Talk About*, "The Bath." I find that when I first read "The Train," I wrote next to its title in the table of contents "a bad story," so I'm guessing I didn't like that one much. I remember liking some of the others, but remember very little specifically about them, while certain stories in *Will You Please* and *What We Talk About* I have never forgotten. That's the fork: if *Cathedral* had been the next Carver book I'd read, I probably wouldn't have bothered to read another book of Carver's.

But reading *What We Talk About When We Talk About Love* changed everything for me.

•

It was quickly clear to me that *What We Talk About* had all the qualities and originality I had admired in *Will You Please*, but it was even more unique, even more severe, the stories cut even closer to the bone. Indeed, several of the stories I felt I intuited more than understood, especially on that first read. There was very little interior space and the dialogue had a higher level of disconnection, as if only the most necessary words were being offered. *Will You Please* felt raw, but *What We Talk About* felt consistently rawer, more instinctual, almost as if the characters were hypnotized or in shock. They seemed at times bewildered, as if they were stumbling through their lives and were not completely sure how they had gotten there. There were few dialogue tags, and when they were there they were generally flat and without modifiers, just *said, said, said* over and over again, or sometimes *I go* in the place of *I say*. A few of the stories (as in *Will You Please*) are told in the present tense and time feels shockingly flattened out as a result. Indeed, the collection as a whole feels consistently stripped down: no wasted words, a great deal of mystery, and readers left to connect many of the dots on their own. Explanation and discursive gestures are cut back more dramatically than in *Will You Please*, which gave me the impression that I was figuring out what was happening at only a slight remove from the characters themselves, sharing a bit of their shock.

The first story, "Why Don't You Dance?", sets the tone for the stories that follow. It opens with the line, "In the kitchen he poured another drink and looked at the bedroom suite in his front yard." (3) Then, rather than explaining why the bedroom suite is in the front yard, it simply describes it. As readers, we've arrived after something has ended, in the aftermath of something, but rather than flashing back to give us details about what happened, we proceed on, gaining slight hints as we go of what might have occured, but never enough to have more than a fragmented picture. The wound is still too raw to be carefully examined. We are operating in a tenuous present that is built on the precarious wreckage of the past. But rather than taking a breath and thinking through what has happened, the unnamed man whose furniture is in his yard would rather get drunk. Better to finish his whiskey and get rid of everything that reminds him of the past.

It's significant too that the gesture that inaugurates *What We Talk About When We Talk About Love* is the pouring of a drink. Not only a drink: *another* drink. That gesture will be repeated again and again, from story to story. Characters attend AA and then backslide, a father dies drunk in his sleep, an estranged wife pours Teacher's scotch over her husband's belly and licks it off. A woman is sleepless beside her passed-out husband; an aging father tells his son over drinks at an airport bar about the particulars of cheating on his mother; two friends leave their wives to have drinks at a VFW bar and then go out and raise hell; a man long sober craves a drink; a group of men sit around a campfire drinking whiskey despite being aware that there's a dead and nude woman floating in the water a few dozen yards away; a man shows up the day after Christmas at his ex-wife's house (after nearly burning down her house the night before) and starts drinking her vodka; four friends sit around a table telling stories about love and getting drunker and drunker, more and more belligerent; a man argues with his daughter about whether he can stop drinking or not, at first trying to hide his full glass from his wife and then defiantly draining it. If there's a constant in these stories, it's that everybody is either drunk, desperate for a drink, or recovering. Many are still injured and degraded by what they've done, which makes them drink more. As the narrator of "Gazebo" says, "When I look back on it, all our important decisions have been figured out when we were drinking. Even when we talked about having to cut back on our drinking, we'd be sitting at the kitchen table or out at the picnic table with a six-pack or whiskey."[9]

I was a Mormon kid. In high school I knew kids, also Mormon, who drank or got high (drugs were far easier to acquire than beer), but I wasn't one of them. The only drink I'd had by the time I read *What We Talk About* was when,

---

9. A page later this same narrator goes on to suggest "Booze takes a lot of time and effort if you're going to do a good job with it." (26) Carver's characters all do a "good job" with it.

at age five, we'd gone to visit my aunt and uncle to find my aunt's father staying with them. It was a hot day and I'd arrived thirsty. He was sitting in an overstuffed chair and there was a tumbler of water on the end table beside him. I ran to it, picked it up and took a big drink, only to discover it wasn't water at all but vodka.

I remember none of that. I only know the story from having heard my parents tell it and talking about how funny my aunt's father thought the expression on my face as I spit the vodka out was, how angry it made my mother that he didn't try to stop me.

But, that being the case, why did these stories appeal to me? On one essential level, these were not people who were "like me." I couldn't relate to the specifics of their situation. And yet, I wasn't reading the stories looking for some kind of affirmation of the deleterious effects of alcohol either (though I do imagine that if you're in recovery, or in denial about needing to be in recovery, *What We Talk About* is a very different book).

But I also believe the importance of having to identify with a character in a book is vastly overrated, particularly when it comes to readers who read fairly broadly. The more you read, the more you realize that reading is about engaging in an act of translation: that you're not looking for someone who is involved in the exact experience or life you have. No, you're more interested in the modality of the experience, and the way in which that modality might reveal things to you about your own, very different experience.

When I was at BYU, I had teachers recommend to me all sorts of Mormon writers, people who had experiences that were, in the basic particulars, quite close to my own. I found this work, on the occasions when I did read it, pretty universally unbearable. On the surface it looked the same as my life, but the apprehension of that experience was quite different. I was, in many ways, a weird Mormon. My parents were both democrats, my father the head of the local democratic party, which was, to say the least, atypical. My experience of being Mormon in Utah was an experience of being very careful about what I said around others, of having to explain constantly when I was in high school how it was possible I could be both Mormon *and* democrat, of having to joke and laugh and interact with people who generally had a very strong sense of how they felt the world and life worked and having that sense be profoundly different from my own. It was having someone tell my girlfriend that I was smart but evil, and that she should break up with me. Living in Utah for me was like always having a low-grade fever, like being constantly under siege.

Growing up, one of the mantras that I heard over and over again was that if you were Mormon you should be "in the world but not of the world." You interacted with the world but always held yourself back, remembered that your first commitment was to your religion. As a Mormon, you were one of God's chosen people and God could choose to speak to you directly at any time, but you should also obey your church leaders unconditionally. Indeed, we were told that if we obeyed our church leaders, even if they misled us, even if they told us to do something wrong, if we did it we would still be blessed.

I did not believe this for a fucking second. Sure, I was in the secular world but not of it, because I was Mormon. But I was also in the Mormon world but not of it, because I didn't fit in. I felt I was in any number of worlds, but I was never of any of them. I didn't slot neatly in anywhere— which, it strikes me, is a very productive place for a writer to be. I had two intelligent parents who insisted that I think for myself. They didn't believe church leaders should be obeyed unconditionally and told me so either through their words (my father, who made no bones about what idiocy he thought it was ever to do something you knew to be wrong because a church leader told you to do it) or through their actions (my mother, who refused to be subservient as so many Mormon women are, and who I remember working actively in support of the Equal Rights Amendment when I was nine or ten, despite the Mormon Church's kneejerk opposition to it). It's probably not a coincidence that all but one of my parents' five children have left the church. We left because we had been encouraged to think for ourselves.

For Dambudzo Marechera—a Zimbabwean writer I stumbled across completely by accident in the BYU library maybe a year after discovering Carver and whose astonishing "The Slow Sound of His Feet" is one of the few stories whose effect on the development of my fictional style I can actually measure[10]—literature is "a unique universe that has no internal divisions. I do not pigeon-hole it by race or language or nation. It is an ideal cosmos co-existing in this one." He goes on to add: "I have been an outsider in my own biography, in my country's history, in the world's terrifying possibilities. It is, therefore, quite natural for me to respond with the pleasure of familiar horror to that section of European literature which reflects this."[11] That idea of "familiar horror" being recognized in something seemingly quite different is exactly what I felt in Carver.

Writers, Marechera suggests elsewhere, not only occupy the nation they live in, but also a country entirely their own, a country populated by writers both living and dead from all parts of the globe. There's something amazing about the fact that my first collection of stories could owe so much to, among others, a Welsh poet who taught me in Utah (and who like me was *in* that very odd Mormon world but even less *of* it), to an anti-authoritarian writer

10. So many of the writers who have become essential to me are writers that I've stumbled across by accident. Marechera was almost as formative an influence on me as Carver; indeed, a story in my first collection, *Altmann's Tongue*, "My Possessions" was inspired by his novella "The House of Hunger" and takes its beginning lines from that piece.

11. Dambudzo Marechera, "The African Writer's Experience of European Literature," *Zambezia* (1987), 99–105.

from Zimbabwe who died penniless from AIDS-related illness, and to an alcoholic writer from Yakima, Washington who died of lung cancer.

Familiar horror. What I saw reading *What We Talk About When We Talk About Love* was a certain attitude, a way of addressing the world, that struck me as specifically spawned from the American West. There was a fatalism to the stories, but also a persistence: not nihilism so much as a way of having to live with, and live on despite, the dangers of the frontier that somehow worked itself into a laconic and stolid approach to life in general. Life sweeps you along and does what it wants to you. Indeed, "Things change, he says. I don't know how they do. But they do without your realizing it or wanting them to." (*What*, 134)

Admittedly, this aspect of the stories was as much my own slightly eccentric reading as it was Carver's intention, a kind of active Bloomian misprision that allowed the work to be for me what I, as a young writer from the American West, needed it to be. Suggests Joan Didion about her reading habits, "I was already given, at sixteen or seventeen, to editing the text as I read it."[12] The same was probably true for me, and perhaps true, to a greater or lesser degree, for all writers, since reading and writing are so intertwined, both being undeniably creative activities. I remember in college having a long conversation with my friend David Beus about Beckett's *Molloy* and explaining what I liked

12. Didion, *Magical Thinking*, 151.

so much about the relation of the two halves of that bifurcated novel, only to have him say "That's interesting, but it's
not actually part of the book." When I read it again, I discovered that yes, he was right, it wasn't in the book. Instead,
my mind was toying with the novel, pushing it in a slightly
different direction for my own purposes.

Good books allow for this. They have a productive
ambiguity that stimulates a creative energy that keeps
them active and alive in a way that books more insistent
on "meaning something" don't manage. There's enough
productive ambiguity in Carver's work, enough absence of
interior space, to allow the reader to fill many details in for
themselves. Where some readers might read that lack of
interior space in *What We Talk About* as a withholding of
information and believe there really is a full emotional interior life to these characters, I saw it instead as very western.
I saw these characters as not being in a position to be able
to reflect fully on their lives, and the moments when they
try (as, say, the girl in "Why Don't You Dance?"), they find
that words won't take them far enough. Indeed, on one level,
What We Talk About When We Talk About Love is a language-
object that intends to express (or try to express) the inade-
quacy of language as a means of expression.

•

I never hunted, but everybody around me did. I remember
going over to a friend's house to find a deer strung up in the

garage, a plastic garbage can positioned beneath it to catch the blood. When in the middle of college I moved off-campus into an apartment with three friends, we lived largely on venison that one of my roommates would periodically bring back in a cooler from his dad's freezer. I fished with my father, and that was vivid for me—immediately upon reading Carver I was convinced he was writing from experience. And the places many of his stories were set in: not precisely the same as the mountains and streams of Utah, but still resonant with my own experience.

Which made me wonder: why was so much of the fiction I was being encouraged to read based in large Eastern cities? And New York in particular? Was it just because publishing was based there? I'd never even been to New York. My only relation to that city was from having read about it in novels. Carver's characters seemed like they could be people I knew. They didn't go to prep schools, they weren't wealthy, they didn't wear tuxedos, they hadn't learned Latin. Instead, they hunted and fished, they drank and smoked. They were a mess, but they were likeable. They sometimes did awful things, but they didn't really seem to know why they did them. Like the people I went to school with, they lived on farms or ranches. They weren't wealthy, but they got by, mostly. They were battered by life, but they survived.

Which, I suppose, suggested to me that I could survive too.

Three

HERE I AM IN MY CAR, IN 2011, AFTER NEARLY DYING IN the hospital, after my girlfriend and I have broken up, listening to the same CD over and over and over again. I am not going to mention what CD it is, simply because if I were to tell you it would be incomprehensible.

Really? Why that? Do you even like that? That doesn't make any sense.

There is only one reason for it being the CD it was: it was the CD I had playing in my car, for no particular reason, on the day my girlfriend and I broke up. I found I could not physically bring myself to take it out of the player. I have no idea how many times I played it. Dozens of times at least, but probably hundreds.

I was playing it over and over again, I suppose, as a way of trying to keep time from continuing on. If the same CD was always playing then we were still at the same day, the same moment, and things might go differently. I might walk out of the car and into the house and handle things quite differently, and then life might go back to being what it was.

The day I knew I was going to be okay was not the day I stopped thinking I saw my girlfriend everywhere I went, not the day when I started seeing someone else, not the day when I discovered my girlfriend and the person I had thought of as my best friend were now secretly seeing one another, but the day I pressed eject and removed that CD.

•

Sometimes we need these moments of familiarity, of stability, as a way of gathering ourselves for a moment, or even longer than a moment, before we go on. Other times we need just the opposite. When I first read *What We Talk About When We Talk About Love*, I didn't need to be soothed, I didn't need something to convince me that things would be the same as they always had been and would never change. I needed just the opposite: a book that would shake me up. That, probably as much as anything else, was why, despite how much "Nobody Said Anything" shocked me, I began to voraciously read Carver.

•

If you want to get a full sense of these stories, how they function thematically, how they cohere and develop, there are other books and articles that already do this and do it better than I, always more a fiction writer than a critic, could manage. What I'm more interested in is trying to give a sense of what specifically I took away from individual stories as a so-called budding writer, the one or two things each individual story showed me. Part of this is, obviously, reconstruction—I read these stories for the first time when I was eighteen and now I'm fifty-one, so nearly thirty-three years have gone by (as an ex-Mormon friend of mine would say, enough time for Christ to be born, replicate some loaves and fishes, and be crucified). But, I do still have the first copy of *What We Talk About When We Talk About Love* that I read, and it still contains my penciled annotations. Because of that, I can see what that eighteen-year-old was paying attention to.

•

I've already talked about "Why Don't You Dance?"—the first story in *What We Talk About*—but I still have a few things to say.

When I first read it, I marked not moments where something significant happens plot-wise, but moments like this: "Why don't you kids dance? he decided to say, and then he said it. 'Why don't you dance?'" (8) Another writer might have chosen to drop that last sentence, thinking "and then he said it" was enough. But Carver's repetition adds humor and the slight variation, both keeps it from being too absurd a repetition and also suggests a disjunction between thought process and speech. He's decided to say something, and then he says it. Only he doesn't say *exactly* what he's decided to say. *Why?* I couldn't help but momentarily wonder. That interaction of repetition and variation is one of the things that Carver does exceptionally well, and at just the right times.

There's also something quite interesting about the temporal rhythm of the story. It's broken into eight short sections (I'd numbered them in my copy as a way, I suppose, to count them), but we're sometimes left on our own to figure out the relationship of the sections to one another—it often takes you a moment of reading to locate yourself. The initial seven sections all take place on the same day. The first of these, however, occurs earlier in the day, and thus is slightly set off from the rest. Sections 2-7, however, are all part of the same scene, the same event. I'd been taught not to break into a new section unless there was a definite shift—a change of place, the entrance of a new character, a movement forward in time, etc. But Carver uses these shifts to allow us to absorb the event in pieces, and to have distinct, chiseled units rather than a single sprawling scene. Each section does its work and then pauses, allowing us to absorb it, and then a new section starts. Maybe some time has passed in the meantime, but we're often not sure exactly how much, or we figure out only as we read further and realize the characters are quite a bit drunker. Carver[13]

13. I use "Carver" here and elsewhere as a shorthand for the author of

establishes a sectional rhythm dependent on something other than shifts in time or place. He is one the first to successfully employ such a strategy, and he's still among of the very best at it.

For me, the most interesting thing about the sectional progression of the story was, and still is, the relation of the eighth and last section to the rest. Here, suddenly, we jump forward: "Weeks later," it begins. The story is around 1600 words long, with the short last section being under 90 words. In other words, almost 95 percent of the story takes place on a single day, and then the last little bit, the short final section, propels us weeks forward. That changes our relationship to the event, first by casting it further into the past and second by showing us that the girl is still thinking about it, still trying to make sense of it, weeks later. Instead of showing us what's going on inside her head at the time, Carver very briefly shows her trying (and failing) to talk about it much later, trying (and failing) to sort it out.

•

"Viewfinder" is a first-person story that begins "A man without hands came to the door to sell me a photograph of my house." The situation seems doubly absurd, and you

---

the stories, though as I'll discuss later it's fairly clear that many of the effects and stylistic gestures that I was drawn to when I was eighteen weren't exclusively the work of Raymond Carver's original writing, but largely due to the revisions of his editor Gordon Lish.

read on partly to see how the logic of the story will unfold. At first the unnamed narrator is only curious—he offers the man coffee, for instance, because he wants to know how, with hooks, he'll manage to hold the cup. But as they talk and the narrator sees how quickly the hook-handed man has him pegged as lonely and abandoned, he decides to have the hook-handed man take multiple pictures of him in front of the house, in various poses. Soon the narrator is up on the roof, throwing rocks as the man below takes snapshots, the latter dubious about whether they will turn out. It's as if the narrator wants to document his presence, to assert himself as being there. As more photos are taken, his desperation turns to a kind of slightly deranged joy. But, of course, we know that once the photo session is done he'll have to come down from the roof and go back into his lonely house. Like "Why Don't You Dance?" there's a displacement here of the inside of the house to the outside. In that story, it's a literal movement of the furniture; in this one, it's the movement of the inhabitant of the house to the roof and yard.

But the main thing I was learning, just two stories in, was that you could write stories in which you never gave the characters names, where you called them just "the man" or "the girl" or "the boy" or even, if they were narrating the story, nothing at all. And that that could still elicit a strong emotional response from a reader.

•

"Mr. Coffee and Mr. Fixit," like "Viewfinder," is one of several stories in the collection that I find less interesting as individual stories but which add significantly to the feel of the collection as a whole, emphasizing certain ideas and gestures seen in other stories. Reading these minor stories, I began to understand the difference between a simple grouping of stories and a larger integrated work, the way the parts of a collection can work together to create a larger, cohesive whole.

At just four pages, "Mr. Coffee and Mr. Fixit" is the second shortest story in the collection—though, as I'll discuss later, before Gordon Lish edited it, it was originally about six times as long. In it, an unnamed narrator describes things he experienced three years before, when he was out of work, drinking heavily, and his wife was cheating on him. The story's tone is conversational, the kind of thing you might hear from a drunken stranger on the barstool next to you. In four quick sections, it wanders through him finding his sixty-five-year-old mother making out on the sofa with a man, his reflections about the man who his wife was having an affair with ("I used to make fun of him. But I don't make fun of him anymore"), and on to mention of his father dying drunk in his sleep. We know little about this narrator's current life, about the place from which he is telling his story, and the story doesn't have a plot exactly. It's more about an individual vocalizing something about their past and us as readers trying to decide what it tells us about them that they chose to tell us these disconnected stories, and tell them in this particular way.

•

"Gazebo" concerns a husband and wife in the process of drinking, fucking, and breaking up. They manage a hotel and he's had sex repeatedly with one of the maids until his wife discovers the affair. Now they've shut down the hotel office and are locked drunk in a room trying to sort out what to do, trying to stay for as long as possible suspended in a drunken moment that will separate their past lives together from their future lives apart. "Gazebo" was most notable to me for being written in the present tense—the first of several such stories in *What We Talk About*—and for the way it often substitutes "I go" or "she goes" in place of "I say" and "she says." That repetition of "go" emphasizing that they both will soon go their separate ways.[14]

That use of present tense is something I think of as characterizing both minimalism and Carver in particular (indeed, rereading the book, I was surprised how few of the stories are actually present tense). It creates a sense of immediacy: you're not reading about something that happened in the past, but something that's happening right

14. Anatole Broyard is less kind to this gesture (and certain others) in his 04/15/1981 review of the collection for the *New York Times*: "The next story, which is about adults, employs an 'I go - she goes' idiom that we reluctantly associate with children. Mr. Carver uses repetition in dialogue in a manner that takes us all the way back to the homely sentimentalism of the 30's, in which the proletariat struggles with language and thought like a beetle on its back, flailing its legs."

now. I probably associate present tense narration with minimalism largely because of William H. Gass's essay excori-
ating minimalism, "A Failing Grade for the Present Tense,"
which mentions "Gazebo." Says Gass of such stories,

> They are stories shorn, not only of adjectives and
> adverbs, but of words themselves, almost as if their
> authors didn't know any. Some warriors arm them-
> selves for battle, but these warriors, like wrestlers,
> strip. They write in strips, too. Sentences are invari-
> ably short, declarative, and as factual as a string of
> fish. Images are out. It is fraudulent to poetize[. . .]
> Kept simple, quick, direct, like a punch, the sen-
> tences avoid subordination, qualification, subtlety.
> Subordination requires judgment, evaluation; it cre-
> ates complexity, demands definition.[15]

All this is more or less true, I suppose, but when I was
first reading it in Carver, not having seen it elsewhere, it felt
fresh and new to me, different from what other writers (or
at least other writers I knew) were doing. If at the time I'd
been better read in contemporary American fiction, I might
not have been struck that way—and indeed, there are many
stories from that tradition that attempt to limp by on style

15. William Gass, "A Failing Grade for the Present Tense" in *Finding a
Form* (New York: Knopf, 1996), 14-30. The original version of this essay,
published in the *New York Times* in 1987, is slightly different in phrasing,
though the substance is the same.

alone. But, yes, it did work for me that first time, and at this point the use of present tense in those stories doesn't feel artificial to me. Rather it's like putting on an old, familiar sweater.

I also realize that enough water has gone under the bridge in the three decades since that there are very few people today who would feel the same impact of reading Carver for the first time, who would be as taken as I was by something like his use of tense. It just wouldn't feel new or daring anymore.

I taught George Saunders' *CivilWarLand in Bad Decline* in my graduate fiction workshop at Oklahoma State University in 1996, just a few months after that book came out. Students loved it: it felt to them (and to me) genuinely different from anything they had read before. Eight or nine years later, at Brown University, I taught it again, expecting the students to love it just as much, but was surprised to find some of them indifferent to the book. "I don't know," said one shrugging student when I asked him why, "it just reminded me too much of other things I've read." When I pressed him about what those other things were, he went on to name writers who had all started publishing after Saunders, all of whom had acknowledged him as an influence, some of whom had even been blurbed by him.

Certain books can fall victim to their own success. They can reorient the literary field in such a way that they no longer feel as original as they once did, largely because they *were* so influential and so other writers have changed the way they write because of them. That is certainly the case with *What We Talk About When We Talk About Love*, which strikes me as the most influential book of fiction of the early 1980s.

But, then again, maybe it's just a question of things going in waves. When I taught Saunders more recently, students were enthusiastic again. That wave of books that were influenced by Saunders had been popular a few years before they were actively reading literary work, so now he felt new again.

•

"I Could See the Smallest Things" is one of only two stories in this seventeen-story collection to be narrated by a woman. These stories appear roughly one third and two thirds of the way through the collection, the first female voice appearing five stories in, the second ten stories in, so we're half-expecting the second when it does appear. Carver has been careful to create a progression from story to story, never grouping together too many stories that are similar. He leads us to expect a kind of rhythm of movement from first to third person, from more meandering tales to more plotted ones, from male to female characters, and so on.

"Smallest Things" is a slice-of-life story. A woman lying in bed next to her passed-out husband thinks she hears her gate open. She tries to wake up her husband and fails, then goes out herself to see what's going on. Outside, she finds her estranged neighbor killing slugs. He tells her that he quit drinking ("Had to. For a while it was getting so I didn't know up from down" (35)), and asks about her husband who he has fought with and who he'd like to be friends with again. Eventually, she goes back inside and lies down.

I've written "I . . . ," "I . . . ," "I . . ." at various points on the first several pages of the story and indeed it is a beginning in which a larger number of sentences begin with "I" than usual: Nearly half of the sentences in the first section begin with "I." Is this a flaw? I don't think so, largely because of how this pattern changes as the story progresses. By the second section, a third of the sentences begin with "I," and there's not the same staccato repetition of similar sentence structures near one another. The next section offers even fewer. The contrast between those declarative and "I"-focused sentences in the beginning with the more varied back and forth between her and her neighbor that follows makes that later conversation seem richer. It also emphasizes her initial loneliness to have the first section repeat "I" over and over again, despite the fact that she's in bed beside her husband.

Small choices, often intuitive, are what make a story succeed or fail. Little adjustments of grammar, little changes in syntax, slight disruptions, all can do a tremendous amount for the overall effect. By contrast, a careless choice can slightly mar the effect that you're trying to produce, can lessen the overall impact. Minimalist fiction gives us ample opportunity to see both small choices that are successful and those that are failures.

•

"Sacks" is another first-person story, told in present tense, the present being in this case the moment in which the story he feels compelled to tell is being passed along to someone else. The narrator, in a hotel room in a Midwestern city (why coy about which city it is?), wants to "pass along" to a "you" (who, exactly?) a story that his father told him at an airport bar about cheating on his mother and how it led to their divorce. I've always found it painful watching adults telling children things they know they shouldn't but can't help themselves. Perhaps it's even more painful for the child. I also know, as a parent who has been divorced, that it can be very hard *not* to tell your children what you find problematic about your ex-, and even try to make them share your opinion. But this story is different, not a condemnation of the mother but more about the father's abjection and misery. The father wants to confess what he did—but not to his wife, to his son. And he's saved this confession just for his son: "I haven't told this to nobody." (43)

What do you do with such a confession? What fascinated me about the story when I first read it was less the story itself—after all, it's a fairly banal infidelity story—but the focus on the moments of telling. First, that the father would feel he can—even should—tell this story to his son, and that the son finds himself compelled to just listen, knowing that his plane will soon arrive and he'll be able to leave. And second, that now the son is passing the story along to "you." It's almost as if the story itself is a virus, spreading from host to host, demanding to be told.

There's also, for the reader, the growing realization that the son might be more like his father than he cares to admit. When the father asks how his wife and children are, the narrator responds that everyone is fine, "which was not the truth." What that means exactly, this version of the story never reveals,[16] but there's at least the implication that the son's own relationship has collapsed as well.

•

And then there's "The Bath," which along with the brutal "Tell the Women We're Going," "So Much Water So Close to Home," and the title story, is among my very favorite stories in the collection. "The Bath" first started life as "A Small, Good Thing," and a partially restored and expanded version of the story would appear in Carver's next collection of stories, *Cathedral*. For me, a student's preference for either "The Bath" or "A Small, Good Thing" serves as a

16. "The Fling," the version of "Sacks" found in *Beginners*, the unedited version of *What We Talk About When We Talk About Love* that appears, among other places, in the Library of America edition of Carver's collected stories, fills in some of the gaps: "Of course, he didn't know we'd been living apart for nearly six months." (789)

litmus test for what their aesthetic preferences as a whole are. If you like "The Bath" you will prefer Carver's first two books. If you like "A Small, Good Thing" you will prefer his later, less severe work. I unabashedly prefer "The Bath," perhaps partly because I read it first. Over the years, I've had countless conversations with my professors, with fellow students, with my own students, with colleagues, with other writers, most (but not all) of whom strongly prefer "A Small, Good Thing." I have listened to their arguments but find I still do not prefer "A Small, Good Thing."

"It's a more human story," one student told me. Yes, I conceded, and that's why I like it less; it doesn't fit my conception of what the world is like as well as "The Bath."

"'A Small, Good Thing,' is still quite stripped down," a PhD student at Oklahoma State told me, "but it's also so much more insightful." But I don't think of it as more insightful. I think of it as more *comforting*. The way I think of "A Small, Good Thing" is that instead of leaving us suspended in agony and difficulty, as "The Bath" does, it offers us a mock sacrament and makes us feel the slight frisson that suggests things might be okay. The way I see it is that when Carver wrote "A Small Good Thing" he looked into the face of the void, and flinched. "The Bath" does not flinch. "No pleasantries," the narrator says about a verbal exchange that occurs within the story, "just this small exchange, the barest information, nothing that was not necessary." (48) That might serve, too, as a description of the strategies of *What We Talk About When We Talk About Love* as a whole.

For me, the most amazing thing about "The Bath" was the place that it ended. The story didn't do the thing that I'd been told stories should do and conform to Freytag's pyramid, with rising action, a climax, falling action and then a denouement. Instead it builds very slowly and then stops at the climax, abandoning us as readers at a point of great tension. I loved what that did to me as a reader, the way it left the story open where it couldn't help but continue to evolve for me after I finished it. I think as a reader that I know who this is calling, that it's the baker, but I don't know for certain. There's the slimmest possibility it might be the person who hit the boy with his car—I know it's not, but I can't help but think of that, because, of course, I know the mother is thinking exactly that.

There's also the sense—not logical, not rational, but still there—that it might be something more metaphysical. Rereading the story for the first time in a long while, I thought of Muriel Spark's wonderful *Memento Mori*, in which aging characters receive mysterious phone messages telling them to "Remember you must die." That novel deliberately chooses not to let us know who, if anyone human, is actually calling.

"The Bath" also provides illustrations of how you can employ the careful description of an action or an act in a way that makes that action or act uncanny. Take for instance this passage: "She took the left arm out from under the covers and put her fingers on the wrist." It's a very distanced way to say "She took his pulse," and ends up making what we think of as a normal action seem very strange, which helps to put us in a place where we can share the mother and father's irrational state of mind.

"The Bath" is best read prior to reading "A Small, Good Thing," since much of the mystery that makes it effective is explained away by the latter. Substantially longer (in the Library of America's *Raymond Carver: Collected Stories* "The Bath" is seven pages while "A Small, Good Thing" is twenty-four pages), it fills everything out that "The Bath" leaves unstated and continues to draw the arc, to complete (admittedly eccentrically) Freitag's pyramid. I'm not suggesting that "A Small, Good Thing" isn't a good story—it has genuine strengths and it is a story I would have been proud to have written—but I remain convinced that "The Bath" is a more inventive story.

Carver, however, was convinced of just the opposite, perhaps primarily because the changes made from "A Small, Good Thing" to "The Bath" are edits and deletions made by Gordon Lish, rather than Carver himself. These changes reflect Lish's sense of the world more than Carver's. In a letter to Lish quoted in the *Collected Stories*, Carver speaks of "A Small, Good Thing" as one of the stories that he isn't willing to let go of, though after a phone conversation with Lish he did in fact allow "The Bath" to be published with Lish's edits.[17] The fact that he would publish "A Small, Good

---

17. Cf. the notes found at the end of Raymond Carver, *Collected Stories* (New York: Library of America, 2009), 990–1004. The letter in question appears on pages 992–96.

Thing" two years later as part of *Cathedral* speaks volumes: Carver wants to have it read in place of "The Bath."[18]

There's an ethical dilemma at stake here, and with me being an author who had Lish as the editor of his first book, I feel that dilemma quite acutely, and will discuss it in some detail further on. But as an eighteen-year-old who didn't know Carver's connection to Lish and didn't know of "A Small, Good Thing," I was very happy to read "The Bath." And, despite the ethical dilemma and complexities of intention that the story can't help but raise once you learn more about its origin, I still think it's a tremendous story, and one I would not want to do without.

•

"Tell the Women We're Going" is about friendship, kind of. It's about two friends who grow up, get families, and begin to lead separate lives. One of them, Bill, is more of a follower. The other, Jerry, is more brash and perhaps, as becomes increasingly clear as the story progresses, unhinged.

---

18. It should be stated that when Carver chose to "restore" this story, he did not restore it to what it was before Lish touched it. Instead he strikes an uneasy compromise (or happy medium?) in which he tries to return to the story's original fullness while still maintaining certain of Lish's cuts. For instance, besides playing with wording, Carver keeps deleted a several-page long flashback in which the mother remembers when her son had been lost and she and her husband had been afraid he had drowned. The *Collected Stories* offers both versions of "A Small, Good Thing" for ready comparison.

It's the story of what happens when Jerry convinces Bill to leave their wives and kids for the afternoon to go have a few drinks, drive around, and eventually chase and tease two young girls. Bill knows things are going wrong, but he keeps letting himself be led forward. The most he can do is glance at his watch and suggest it might be time to go back. By the end of the story, Jerry has killed both girls, leaving Bill in a terrible dilemma.

"Tell the Women We're Going" does the same thing that "The Bath" does in terms of ending abruptly, at a point of tension. But it also truncates and speeds up dramatically at the end, with the murder of the girls being covered in a single sentence. Carver chooses to have the murder occur abruptly and shockingly before Bill (and us) even sees it coming. Indeed, we don't know that Jerry is going to kill the girls until the final sentence of the final paragraph. That paragraph reads in full:

> He never knew what Jerry wanted. But it started and ended with a rock. Jerry used the same rock on both girls, first on the girl called Sharon and then on the one that was supposed to be Bill's. (66)

"Why Don't You Dance?" balances the day covered in its first seven sections against the weeks that follow as discussed in its eighth section, but we tend to accord these two parts an equivalent narrative weight because of the way they function as similar units of time. In "Tell the Women We're

Going" we leave the story feeling that the last couple of paragraphs really constitute the second half of the story and that had they been told with a little bit of detail[19] could have been almost as long as the rest of the story. That's often the literary strategy with violent moments: time slows down. It seems to move more slowly than the narrative as a whole, the scenes described with a certain amount of either detail or metaphor or both.[20] You might, for instance, compare the ending of "Tell the Women We're Going" with the way in which Cormac McCarthy depicts Sylder's one-armed strangling of Kenneth Rattner in *The Orchard Keeper*.[21] There's still confusion and abruptness—you only figure out what's happening as Sylder himself does—but there's also a wealth of detail. Indeed, the scene goes on for three dense pages. But the brutal abruptness of Carver's ending does an even better job of leaving the reader reeling, and leaving the details of the murders to the imagination.

•

"After the Denim" covers very different territory. It's a story about an elderly couple who go to bingo night only to find their usual seats taken by a hippy couple who seem to be

19. As, indeed, they are in the original version of the story.
20. Something similar happens with movies: think of all the slow-motion shoot-outs that you find in action films.
21. Cormac McCarthy, *The Orchard Keeper* (New York: Vintage, 1965), 37–40.

cheating and who eventually win a cash prize. James Packer is a recovering alcoholic, though there are only a few hints in the story to make it clear this is the case—but the predominance of that struggle in other stories with other characters makes these hints stand out. During the evening, his wife discovers that she's spotting, and that she may be going through something serious physically. They are facing their own mortality in very different ways, with James resenting the hippies and wanting to "set those floosies straight!" (77) and his wife wanting to be alone. The shift to such a story is a nice contrast to the story that came before (and will be as well for the story that comes after).

"After the Denim" left me cold, perhaps because of my youth, when I first read it. Even now, over fifty, I find it a story that I admire abstractly, but don't really care for—it paints its contrasts with a little too broad of a brush. I've thought in the past that it's a story that could have been left out without hurting the collection, but it does add thematic facets that other stories don't have. In any case, this is one of the stories that functions better as part of the collection as a whole than as an individual piece.

•

"So Much Water So Close to Home" is another murder story, though in this case the murder floats in the background of a larger story of the relationship of a wife to her husband. Told from the wife's perspective, it is the story of her husband and three friends going on a fishing trip and finding a young woman's dead body floating in the river. Rather than calling the police, they decide to set up camp, tying the girl to a branch with a rope to keep her from floating away. For two days, they stay and play cards, fish, and drink whiskey, only at the end of their trip hiking down to call the sheriff. The husband when he returns doesn't bother to tell his wife this, just comes home and coaxes her into sex; she finds out about the dead body only later, once it is mentioned in the paper the next day and reporters begin calling the house.

"So Much Water" is the story of a wife's suspicions and her identification with this girl who has been murdered and then left to float so that some men can get on with their fishing. It is a story of simple, even thoughtless male brutality, and about those moments that make you reevaluate your marriage, and also about a woman's struggle to adapt to her changing sense of what the world is and who her husband is. The opening of the story—"My husband eats with a good appetite. But I don't think he's really hungry."—sets a kind of pattern of scrutiny, with the wife judging how her husband appears on the surface but trying to see through that to who he really is. The ending, too, in which she seems to have taken on quite directly the identity of the dead girl, I find stunning.

•

"The Third Thing That Killed My Father Off" is essentially a fish story with a dark edge, about a mute man called

Dummy who ships in bass to Washington state to stock his pond, but then once the pond is stocked can't bring himself to let anyone fish it. It's got more of a humorous edge than a lot of Carver's stories, but there's a grimness there too. It's told by the son of a man who is (or rather was) Dummy's friend, and has a wonderfully rambling quality to it. It contains gestures like this: "I'll tell you what did my father in. The third thing was Dummy, that Dummy died. The first thing was Pearl Harbor. And the second thing was moving to my grandfather's farm near Wenatchee." There was a great deal of delight for me in that deliberate rearrangement of order of the list of three things, and that gesture is something that informs the story as a whole. Indeed, rereading the book as a whole now, my satisfaction in it comes in the pleasure I get out of these small gestures, slight linguistic irregularities that say something about the situation or about the character telling the story.

Here, as in "Nobody Said Anything," I find much that is convincing about the descriptions of fishing. It has an oral quality that reminds me of listening to friends of my father talking about their fishing trips when I was growing up. For instance, rainbow trout and brook trout are just "rainbow" and "brook," whether they're singular or plural. That small detail makes the story feel decidedly western and working class to me, and does more to convince me of its authenticity than any long technical description of the act of fishing would do. Add to that the language the father uses as he advises his son as he attempts to land a bass, and I'm utterly convinced by Carver's authority: at this point he can tell me anything and I'm likely to believe him. I've never been a strong believer in the maxim "write what you know"—that seems to me too often a way to keep writers confined to a particular geographical, economic or ethnic box—but I do believe that whatever you write, however far from your own experience, you should write with authority and attention. As Henry James says in "The Art of Fiction", "Try to be one of the people on whom nothing is lost!" You say "brook" to me instead of "brook trout," and it reinvokes a whole world, one I haven't inhabited for thirty-five years and which, without Carver's help, I might have forgotten.

•

Burt, in "A Serious Talk," shows up at his ex-wife's house the morning after he's ruined her and his children's Christmas. He wants to apologize. Instead, he pours himself a glass of vodka, interrogates her about the new brand of cigarettes he finds stubbed out, cuts her telephone line when he decides she's talking to her new boyfriend, and eventually walks out with her makeshift ashtray. What makes the story interesting is the way in which Burt seems to have little emotional response to what he's experiencing—even to what he's instigating. It's almost as if he's doing these things just to see what will happen, as if he's numbed and operating at a remove from his own actions. It's at once tragic and absurdly funny watching him do more and more damage and still not quite react verbally as his wife becomes upset and kicks him out yet again. The stripped-down style helps the story hold a delicate balance, not allowing it either to become too blackly comic or too sentimentally tragic.

It's a story I don't think I liked much when I originally read it—it's one of the few stories with no marginalia at all—but it's a story that's grown on me as I've gotten older and recognized perhaps too frequently in myself that strange disconnection of watching yourself do something that you know you shouldn't do, vaguely curious to see what will happen. Unfortunately, as both Burt and I know, the outcome is never good.

•

"The Calm" begins "I was getting a haircut." Like several of Carver's stories in this collection and in *Will You Please*, the focus is on telling stories, and on the way in which the story doesn't always express what the teller believes it will. The once-again unnamed narrator is an outsider, but not too far outside. He and the barber know one another well enough for the barber to recognize him and remember he likes to fish, but they are not well acquainted enough to call one another by name. The others in the barber shop seem to have a closer relation.

One man tells a hunting story about gut-shooting a deer and then pursuing it before giving up. This story upsets an older man, who tells him that he "ought to be out there right now looking for that deer instead of in here getting a haircut." (119) This leads to an argument and almost to blows. Eventually the three men waiting for a haircut, offended, leave. Only the barber and the narrator, the latter already in the chair, are left.

It's a funny story, one that reveals the thin-skinnedness of a certain sort of gruff man. In a way, it's also a story about etiquette, particularly the etiquette of hunting and about what you do or don't say to other men, and about how you say it. If it ended there, it'd just be another slice of life story, but the story goes on to an odd final, sensual moment, with the barber finishing the cut and then running his fingers through the man's hair "tenderly, as a lover would." (121) We discover, too, that this is the moment that the narrator, trying to decide if he's going to remain with his wife, decides to leave. The story ends with the narrator describing the calm he feels both because of his decision and because of the "sweetness" of the fingers moving through his hair. It's a swerve that reorganizes our sense of the story. Titling the story "The Calm" when the words "the calm" only come up in the last paragraph ends up giving that final moment a prominence and weight that allows it to stand up against the humorous portions of the story.

It's a wonderful final section. And it's intriguing that this late in the collection, using essentially the same tools that he has used in the other stories, Carver is still capable of making gestures that surprise me.

•

It occurs to me that there's more humor (albeit often a fatalistic humor) in the last half of the collection than there is in the first, and that this humor ends up both affirming a kind of colloquial voice and a certain western attitude. It also allows the reader a certain amount of subtle relief. Without the humor of these stories, the collection would feel too ponderous, too deliberately bleak.

"Popular Mechanics" structures itself as an extended joke gone wrong, with the last line functioning as a punch line and the title a sly wink. It's a kind of response to the story of Solomon having to decide which of two disputing women is the mother of a baby, but instead of two mothers, it's an estranged couple who are fighting over the baby and end up apparently pulling it apart. Only two pages long, it's also the most absurd of the pieces in the book, and the only one that has a slightly fantastical edge. Strangely enough, the most fantastical story in *Will You Please Be Quiet, Please?*, "The Father" is also the shortest story in that collection. It's as if Carver can only bring himself to wriggle out of the realistic tradition for short periods.[22]

•

22. This might be compared to Gordon Lish's 190-page novel *Extravaganza*, which is subtitled "A Joke Book" and which is an extended vaudeville routine in which the jokes and routines keep going wrong and ending in slaughter. Lish seems to adapt much more naturally to the joke gone wrong, and to absurdity.

"Everything Stuck to Him," as I mentioned earlier, is my least favorite story, but it does serve a purpose. It's the only story located outside of the United States, the only story that seems to be located in a future in which the character can look back on past difficulty from a vantage of safety. He does so in this story with tenderness, telling his daughter a story about when she was a new baby and he and his wife were young. It's a melancholy story and as such it does something that none of the other stories do.

What makes *What We Talk About When We Talk About Love* such a good collection is not that every story in it is a great story. Indeed, from my perspective, only about half the stories stand up well on their own. But 1) the ones that do stand on their own are quite exceptional and 2) the stories as a whole are working together to create a complex and layered view of abject lives—every story adds to this vision in a different way. Minimalism is often faulted for a lack of complexity, but I think *What We Talk About* is an excellent example of how repetition and variation between stories can in fact create a different kind of nuanced complexity over the course of the collection. When I first read *What We Talk About*, I read it in a single sitting. I just reread it in the same way and found it quite powerful. Because the stories are in conversation with one another, I remain convinced that that's the very best way for the book to be read.

•

The title story of the collection is probably Carver's best known and most read story, though "Cathedral" is doubtless not too far behind. Indeed, just as with "The Bath" and "A Small, Good Thing" (but to a lesser degree), if you have more of a preference either for "Cathedral" or "What We Talk About When We Talk About Love" it's pretty easy to tell what sort of Carver reader you are, whether you prefer a more expansive hopeful Carver or a more minimal, slightly bleaker Carver.

If you've read this far, it's no doubt clear to you which sort of Carver reader I am.

"What We Talk About When We Talk About Love" is a story in which nothing happens beyond people sitting around and talking. What they talk about, as the title suggests, is love. Or, actually, it's not about four people talking so much as people drinking together, talking and drinking, with what they're willing to say shifting as they drink more, hidden feelings coming out. One couple, Mel and Terry, has been together for a while, the other, Nick and Laura, is fairly new to one another. The talk touches on romantic love, insane love, truly deep love, the lack of love, chivalry, ex-wives, etc. The conversation ends not because the subject has been exhausted or anything has been solved about love—indeed, this is one of those recurring conversations that people return to again and again despite making little if any progress—but because it has grown dark and because, in Mel's words, "Gin's gone." His wife's response to this is "Now what?" (154)

The story has a lovely ending, with the characters sitting in the dark, quite drunk, but still feeling connected—at least if the experience of the narrator, Nick, is shared by the others. Says Nick: "I could hear my heart beating. I could hear everyone's heart. I could hear the human noise we sat there making, not one of us moving, not even when the room went dark." (154) "Human noise" strikes me as being as good a phrase as any for what Carver hopes to get across in these stories as a whole, the human experience in all its glory and ugliness.

There's something stagey but nonetheless effective about this story, with each character having their role and place in the discussion, each representing a different sort of position or ideal in relation to love, based on their own experience. They are embodied ideas. Mikhail Bakhtin talks about one of Fyodor Dostoevsky's strengths being the way in which he "represents every thought as the position of a personality . . . Through this concrete consciousness, embodied in *the living voice of an integral person,* the logical relation becomes part of the unity of a represented event." (9–10) He goes on to say "Each novel presents an opposition, which is never canceled out dialectically, of many consciousnesses, and they do not merge in the unity of an evolving spirit." [23] In other words, what makes Dostoevsky's novels great for Bakhtin is the way that each character is a distillation of a

23. Mikhail Bakhtin, *Problems of Dostoevsky's Poetics,* Trans. Caryl Emerson (Minneapolis: University of Minnesota Press, 1984).

way of thinking in the form of a character. The point is not to come to some kind of resolution in which one position wins out or in which a kind of synthesis occurs, but to allow each voice to speak fully in its own terms.

Carver's story does that for me. It is about the articulation of ideas about love from different perspectives, and then, once that articulation is complete, the voices fall silent. They can resume again at any time, partly because they are clearly enough defined that we can imagine what they will go on to say. Terri and Mel will never agree on what love is—for Terri, wanting to kill someone because you're crazy about them is love, for Mel "If you call that love, you can have it." (142) But they'll no doubt keep having that conversation again and again, whenever they have enough to drink and are in the right company. Mel will remain a romantic about love in a way that Terri can respect but not share. Nick and Laura will remain sweetly in love until the day when, as time passes, that love becomes more complex or falls apart. Perhaps they will become like Terri and Mel, and a new young couple that was more like them will come to dinner one night and the conversation will repeat but with each of them taking a different side. Or perhaps they'll begin to articulate other, so far unexpressed ideas about love based on their embodied experience.

The point is that the conversation as a whole won't get anywhere, but we'll keep on making our human noise, our ideas glancing off one another as we drink and fall in love and struggle from one day to the next.

"What We Talk About When We Talk About Love" holds up very strongly on its own. That's one reason that it is the title story of the book. The other reason is that it brings together threads from all the different stories, touches on things that have circulated in the other stories but in a more idea-driven way, moving one to a clearer understanding of why all these stories are together and what, as a whole, this book is trying to do. When I read the book for the first time, this was the story that made the whole seem like more than just the sum of its parts. It's nicely placed, too. If it had come earlier in the book, I would have read the rest of the stories from its perspective in advance, which might have made it feel too thematic. Better to have it make things cohere retroactively. At the same time, if it had been the very last story, it would have had too much authority, been too thematically pointed. We would have felt like we'd "gotten somewhere." And of course we have, but the characters both have and haven't, which is why Carver chooses instead to end by taking us away from civilized drunken table conversation and drop us back into the floundering world.

•

The final story, "One More Thing," concerns L.D., whose wife Maxine has come home from work to find him "drunk again and being abusive to Rae," their fifteen-year-old daughter. So she tells him to get out. We're right back in the heart of difficulty, years away from the moment where life is peaceful or the past seen from a safe distance. When he's told to get out, L. D. picks up a jar of pickles and hurls it through the kitchen window. Not out of violence exactly—though that's the way his family sees it. More as a way of just seeing (as we saw in an earlier story) what will happen.

What happens is that he fills his suitcase with everything he can find, and gets ready to leave. But he wants the last word, wants to get something across. At the end of the story:

> He said, "I just want to say one more thing."
>
> But then he could not think of what it could possibly be. (159)

Like "What We Talk About When We Talk About Love" the story ends with silence, but in the place of feeling a kinship in the beating of everyone's hearts, we have a very different kind of human noise here, and silence as frustration. L.D. is left wordless and about to be expelled from his family, but has a long way to go before he'll be able to pull himself together and make sense of this moment. Carver ends the collection with difficulty and rupture rather than connection or satisfaction.

But, paradoxically (perhaps perversely), I find it much more satisfying that he does.

Four

MY INITIAL LOVE OF CARVER'S FIRST TWO BOOKS WAS based simply on the words on the page, on the stories themselves. Besides the short biographical notes that appeared in the books, I didn't know anything about Carver as an individual. This wasn't a time when you could Google someone; it took a little effort to track that sort of information down. I *had* heard a tape of his voice—that was my first introduction to his work after all—and that no doubt had some influence on how I read the stories, but that was it. I hadn't come across the stories in the magazines they had appeared in simply because I wasn't reading literary magazines at the time. I had no sense of the other writers publishing in similar places who might be argued to have a similar aesthetic, no sense of people like Richard Ford or Bobbie Ann Mason or Ann Beattie or Tobias Wolff or any number of others. I read Carver through the light of writers I did know well, like Kafka and Beckett. That still strikes me as an effective way to read Carver, though also an eccentric way, and one that most readers would not share.

But Carver did have several contexts. That group of writers who first started publishing in the 1970s was one context. It is one that gets discussed in many of the articles and books on Carver. There was another context, more covert, that only came fully to light a few years after Carver's death.

•

When I was at BYU there was a professor there named Darrell Spencer. I never had a class from him, but I got to know him quite well later, when I came back to teach at BYU after finishing graduate school in 1994, and got to admire the care and precision with which he constructed his stories. I don't know why I never took a class from Darrell—conflicts in schedule, I suppose, partly, but it might also have been a side effect of running through the course sequence so quickly and of having had a teacher, Leslie Norris, who was willing to keep working with me on my fiction whether I was enrolled in a class with him or not.

Like me, Darrell eventually left BYU, moving first to Ohio State University and then to Southern Utah University where he still teaches. I believe I first met him briefly in 1985, largely because Leslie Norris has told him about my work. Then in December of 1985, after finishing the first semester of my second year at BYU, I took a leave from school and left on a Mormon mission to France and Switzerland.

I was not a great missionary. My first companion and I ended up spending more time enjoying France than we did proselytizing. Eventually both he and I would be sent home for breaking mission rules. He would be excommunicated, and I, my transgressions considered less serious, would be sent to complete my mission in Wisconsin. I did not complete my mission, but instead after six months just walked out one day. Because I had not finished my mission, I wasn't allowed to reenroll at Mormon-run BYU. I would eventually be provisionally readmitted, I was told, but not until after the time my mission would officially have ended.

But that's a story that belongs elsewhere.

•

When I started back to school in early 1988, I befriended a number of students who were working with Darrell Spencer, all of whom referred to him by his first name. From them I found out that while I was away on my mission a new innovative literary magazine called *The Quarterly* had appeared. Only a few issues had been published so far, but Darrell had a story in the first issue, and I believe he'd had stories accepted for later issues as well. Plus, the editor had encouraged Darrell to have his best students send their work his way. One student, I no longer remember who, had been accepted, and that had energized everyone else. It was a real honor to appear there, they told me: the magazine was published by Vintage and had wide distribution, and plus it was edited by Gordon Lish.

"Who's Gordon Lish?" I asked.

They turned to look at me, appalled.

•

I was quickly informed about who Lish was, and once they'd told me I was surprised I hadn't known. Lish was famous, I was told, for editing Raymond Carver. In fact, he'd essentially "discovered" Carver, making friends with him back when they both lived in San Francisco, and then later publishing him in *Esquire* magazine. Before that, from 1961 to 1965, he'd had a little magazine called *Genesis West* where he'd published a variety of writers: Donald Barthelme, Tillie Olsen, Grace Paley, Gina Berriault, among others, all writers who by that time I'd read and admired. Once he became a book editor, Lish had also published Carver's books.[24]

I don't remember if I was told all this at once or just bits and pieces of it and was later to piece the rest of it together on my own, over a number of years. Probably the latter. By the time I had graduated from Brigham Young University and was beginning to attend University of Washington to

24. The best critic on Carver's relationship to Lish is biographer Carol Sklenicka, who wrote *Raymond Carver: A Writer's Life* (New York: Scribner, 2009). In this exhaustive biography, she discusses in some detail Lish's relationship to Carver across the years, a relationship that most others gloss over or minimize.

work on a PhD in English Literature and Critical Theory, I knew a lot more. I was aware that Gordon Lish had a great deal to do with Raymond Carver becoming a successful, published, and widely admired short story writer, and that he was more involved in Carver's success than most editors were with their authors. As David Swanger points out in *Remembering Ray*, the turning point for Carver came because in the early seventies "Gordon Lish had taken an interest in Ray's career. Not just a story or two, but Ray's *career*." [25] Adam Meyer further suggests that "Lish believed in Carver when no one else did, and it was largely through his efforts that the wider world became aware of Carver's skills." [26]

Indeed, Lish gave Carver his first major magazine publication when he accepted "Neighbors" for *Esquire*. In addition, while working at *Esquire*, Lish convinced book publisher McGraw-Hill to allow him to edit and publish under their imprint Carver's first book of stories, *Will You*

25. David Swanger, "No Blessed Calm" in William Stull and Maureen Carroll, eds. *Remembering Ray* (Santa Barbara: Capra Press, 1993). 80–84.

26. Adam Meyer, *Raymond Carver* (New York: Twayne, 1995). Lish's own recent statement about this only partly suggests a belief in Carver: "I saw in Carver's pieces something I could fuck around with. There was prospect there, certainly. The germ of the thing, in Ray's stuff, was revealed in the catalogue of his experience. It had that promise in it, something I could fool with and make something new seeming." (205). Cf. Gordon Lish, "The Art of Editing No. 2," *The Paris Review* 215 (Winter 2015), 194–217.

Please Be Quiet, Please. Lish, when subsequently an editor at Alfred A. Knopf, would go on to publish Carver's next two major books, *What We Talk About When We Talk About Love* and *Cathedral.* Something less well known, but revealed in the Carver correspondence found in Bloomington's Lilly Library and mentioned by Carol Sklenicka, is that when Lish could not get a Carver story accepted at *Esquire* he would often arrange to have it sent to editors of other magazines; that Lish arranged an agent for Carver; that Lish read Carver's stories on the radio to publicize him; and that sometimes Lish engaged a typist for Carver's revisions. Lish would seem to have been a promoter, editor, and publicity agent rolled into one, bringing Carver attention he would not have had otherwise.

In other words, without Gordon Lish I likely would never have read Carver's stories.

•

The other young writers around me at BYU kept sending their work off to Lish's *Quarterly* but for some reason, I never did. Why? Partly because I wasn't crazy about at least some of the writers who were sending; they seemed cliquish to me and I didn't always care much for their work, which seemed to me at times almost a parody of Carver—full of minimalist gestures but without the impact that Carver's work had. That, in my opinion, was one of the difficulties with taking Carver as a model: aspects of his work were easy to imitate, but the imitators rarely came up with anything half so good.

Another reason was that I began to get a sense of what Lish was doing to their stories. I remember sitting in on several conversations where writers had sent a story to Lish and had received it back dramatically marked up, often substantially cut. When one wrote back declaring he didn't agree with the changes, Lish promptly rejected the story. Even the ones who did agree to the changes and sent Lish back a clean revised copy often found a newly marked up version a few days later in the mail. Even if they accepted those revisions, it wasn't certain the story would be taken. I remember an awards dinner at which several of those writers and myself were present. I'd won an award for my poetry—which, frankly, was never great—beating out my classmate Tim Liu, who would go on to publish a number of very fine books of poetry and who now teaches at William Paterson University. I won entirely because there was a line limit to the contest and the judge decided to count lines and disqualify anybody who had exceeded this limit, which every good poet, Tim included, had done.

At the awards dinner I sat next to two students who had won prizes in the fiction category, one of whom had just had a story accepted in the *Quarterly* by Lish. The other was congratulating him. They'd workshopped the story in Darrell Spencer's class and the student kept praising a certain scene in the story, the content of which I no longer remember, seeing this was thirty years ago and I'd never read the story myself. Finally the first student, growing increasingly uncomfortable, admitted, "That scene's no longer in it."

"Why not?" the second student asked.

After hemming and hawing, he admitted that Lish had cut the scene out.

"The whole scene? I mean, that was like half of the story."

The first student nodded and began to talk unconvincingly about why the scene had to go. It was clear he still liked it.

"You should talk Lish into letting you keep it," the second student said. "It's a better story with it in there."

But it was clear that the first student was too nervous that if he didn't accept Lish's changes the story simply wouldn't be published. "It's a good publication," he tried to tell himself. "I can restore the story once I publish it in a collection. It doesn't always have to be like that."

Knowing that Lish had published Carver, my mind immediately went to Carver's "The Bath" and "A Small, Good Thing." Why, I had wondered at the time of reading "A Small, Good Thing," had Carver felt the need to publish two versions of the same story so close together in time?

That was the moment when I first began to seriously wonder how extensively Lish had edited Carver.

•

I knew already that there were different versions of some of the Carver stories. Once I'd read *Will You Please Be Quiet, Please?* and *What We Talk About When We Talk About Love*, I read all of Carver's work I could get my hands on. Despite not liking it as much as those first two books, there was enough to keep me going until I had exhausted it. I had read *Fires* in 1987, oddly enough buying it, a note inside the cover reminds me, on the way to see Tengiz Abuladze's film *Repentance*. The majority of that book consists of essays and poems and a *Paris Review* interview, but it also contains seven stories. Four of the stories—"The Lie," "The Cabin," "Harry's Death," and "The Pheasant"—were stories that hadn't been collected before. Three others—"Distance," "Where Is Everyone?" and "So Much Water So Close to Home"—I recognized from *What We Talk About When We Talk About Love*.

In many circumstances, if I encountered again a story that I'd read relatively recently, I would just skip over it. But in this case, perhaps largely because I'd felt the experience of reading *What We Talk About When We Talk About Love* as a book was greater than the experience of reading the individual stories, I read *Fires* from one end to the other.

I was . . . confused. The stories weren't like I remembered them. There were scenes I didn't recall at all, and even moments of language that were quite different from how I remembered. In "So Much Water So Close to Home" there was backstory that I actually was *certain* hadn't been in the original, including information that the female narrator had spent some time in a clinic. When I compared these versions to the versions in *What We Talk About*, I realized I had been right: the stories in *Fires* were substantially different, fuller, dramatically longer. "Mr. Coffee and Mr. Fixit" had become "Where Is Everyone?" and now was about five times as long. The *Fires* versions also, in my opinion, weren't better. What was going on?

Carver has an afterword to *Fires* in which he gives an explanation of sorts. "I like to mess around with my stories. I'd rather tinker with a story after writing it, and then tinker some more, changing this, changing that, than have to write the story in the first place . . . Rewriting for me is not a chore—it's something I like to do."[27] He goes on to mention that two of the stories, "So Much Water So Close to Home" and "Distance," were originally included in a small press volume of eight stories, *Furious Seasons*, that was published by Capra Press about a year and a half after *Will You Please Be Quiet, Please?* appeared, but then later "largely rewritten" for inclusion in *What We Talk About When We Talk About Love*. Claims Carver,

> After some deliberation, I decided to stay fairly close to the versions as they first appeared in the Capra Press book, but this time hold the revisions to a minimum. They *have* been revised again, but not nearly so much as they once were . . . But I can say

27. Raymond Carver, *Fires: Essays, Poems, Stories* (New York: Vintage, 1984).

now I prefer the later versions of the stories, which is more in accord with the way I am writing short stories these days.

Indeed, for Carver this is "an instance in which I am in the happy position of being able to make the stories better than they were. At least, God knows, I *hope* they're better. I think so anyway." (219)

This confused me for several reasons. *I* wasn't convinced that those stories were better in this new form—they seemed to accomplish just about the same thing but to do so at a more leisurely pace, with less economy, less skill, and less focus. They felt less like the Carver I knew and more like stories that didn't have his distinctive imprint. "So Much Water" was pretty good in both versions (even though I liked the *What We Talk About* version better), but this new version of "Distance" frankly felt interminable to me. Was I to see these as the new definitive versions, to replace the stories as they stood in *What We Talk About?* Or when Carver spoke of preferring the later versions of the stories was he just talking about the original versions in *Furious Seasons* as opposed to these versions? What even constituted a "later" version? He'd acknowledged that these were, in a sense, *in between* versions, going back to an earlier version and revising it so it was somewhere between the version found in *Furious Seasons* and the version found in *What We Talk About?* Why would I prefer them.

And then there was "Where Is Everyone?" Carver didn't even acknowledge that it was a dramatically expanded version of "Mr. Coffee Mr. Fixit." Why not? The colophon did mention that "Where Is Everyone?" was from *What We Talk About*, but not what story it was. This, despite Carver clearly acknowledging in the same colophon note that "Distance" and "Everything Stuck to Him" *are* the same story. Did he hate "Mr. Coffee and Mr. Fixit" that much, to not want to point out the connection?

I'd read *Cathedral* a few years before, so I did have a sense of what he meant by these versions being "more in accord with the way I am writing short stories these days"— they did feel more like those later stories. But what an odd thing to claim you are writing something closer to the style of what you're writing now by taking a revised story and making it more like something you wrote long ago.

It made it feel like Carver's style was on a rollercoaster ride. First it was less full in *Will You Please Be Quiet, Please?* then it was fuller in *Furious Seasons*, then at its most minimal in *What We Talk About When We Talk About Love*, then more expansive again in *Fires*, and finally its most expansive in *Cathedral*.[28] Maybe some of those shifts could be explained by stories written earlier being published later,

28. *Where I'm Calling From* wouldn't be published until a few months later, in 1988. The seven new stories in that book most resemble the work in *Cathedral*. Adam Meyer presents a similar idea, seeing Carver's career as taking the shape of an hourglass: longer stories, then minimal ones, then longer again. Cf. Adam Meyer, "Now You See Him, Now You Don't, Now You Do Again: The Evolution of Raymond Carver's Minimalism," *Critique* (Summer 1989): 239–251.

or by Carver trying to adapt earlier stories to his later style, but it still seemed muddled and confusing to me. *Will You Please* and *What We Talk About* had felt unified, and had functioned so well as collections. *Cathedral* did too, but it was a little less relentlessly unified than *What We Talk About*. *Furious Seasons* and *Fires* were all over the place. Maybe there was something I wasn't seeing.

But I suspected, from the way Lish was editing my fellow students at BYU, that the changes in Carver's style were due to Lish's editing.

Five

IN AUGUST OF 1989, I GRADUATED FROM COLLEGE, turned twenty-three, got married, and moved to Seattle to start graduate school at University of Washington, all in the course of a month. Now, almost thirty years later, twenty-three seems like an astoundingly young age to get married, but at the time, going to BYU and immersed in Mormon culture and unable to live with a woman if I wanted to remain Mormon, it did not. The majority of Mormons my age were not only married, but had been already married for a year or two. A number of them even had children.

My wife Connie and I moved to Seattle and into student married housing. I had applied late and had gotten in at the last minute, largely because Leslie Norris had previously taught at University of Washington and he was able to call and talk them into admitting me. But that meant I was admitted without a teaching position and would have to pay full tuition.

Connie hadn't quite graduated yet from BYU, and ended up taking correspondence courses to finish. She worked in a bank while I started the graduate MA program in English Literature. Mornings I worked at By George, a café on campus, making drinks at the coffee bar. To say I was in over my head is a severe understatement: growing up Mormon, I hadn't actually ever even tasted coffee. When my manager realized this was the case, she assigned me to take orders and work the till. I would ring up an order, take the money, walk to the espresso machine, and write down what the person wanted for the barista (a word I wasn't remotely aware of at the time). That went well for about ten minutes, until someone asked for a café au lait and, not knowing what that was, I wrote down "café olé." Soon I was moved over to work the grill.

Evenings, Connie and I worked two or three times a week in a movie theater, the Guild 45th, and then spent the other nights going to free movies. Between my two jobs and the classes I was taking, I was swamped but still trying to find time to write. I had converted one of the two closets in our aging one-bedroom apartment into a writing space—I could just fit a chair and a secondhand desk into it. It was a tight and claustrophobic space, but it was better than nothing.

I was becoming ambivalent about my relationship to Mormonism and largely went to church to please my wife. And then, out of the blue, I was asked by church leaders if I'd accept a calling to be the second counselor in a bishopric and found myself saying yes. So, on top of everything else, I was one of three people running a congregation of several hundred people, with commitments all day Sunday and at various times during the week as well.

Considering how heavy my course load was, there should have been no time to write fiction, but somehow there was, though that often meant sleeping just four or five hours a night. Being a member of the bishopric meant, I discovered, that I had access to the church's computer and, more importantly, the church's printer, both of which resided in an office to which only a few of us had a key. The office was a great deal more expansive than my closet at home, and the church was only two blocks from our apartment, so often, after my wife was asleep, I'd walk down and work from around ten or eleven until two in the morning.

I finished a number of stories that way and began to send them out. Most came back, but a few were published. I also managed, during that first year of graduate school, to finish work on a novel, called *Siege*.

I use the term "novel" loosely. *Siege* was never a novel. It was just 29,000 words and only about eighty pages long. It was about an odd group of misfits living in a desert fortress, one of whom goes crazy and seals the fortress down, shooting anybody who tries to leave. The others slowly starve to death, go crazy themselves, wander around in underground caves, and so on. I would publish three modified excerpts from it as stories in my first book, *Altmann's*

Tongue (the parts I felt worth saving) but it has otherwise remained unpublished.[29]

But at the time, I felt sure it was a novel and was proud of it. I wanted to send it out. To know where to send my short fiction I had relied on *Writer's Market*, and I did the same with *Siege*. The edition I looked at had a short single-page interview with Ashbel Green, an editor at Knopf who would later publish several of Gabriel García Márquez's books. He seemed interesting and as good a place to start as any, and so I mailed my manuscript to him.

•

A few weeks later, I had a note back from Green, no manuscript attached. He thanked me for sending it. It was not, he said, for him, but he had passed it along to another editor who it might be a better fit for.

I don't believe I was given the name of the editor. I wrote back thanking Green and then settled back hoping to hear from this new editor. After a week with no word, I became caught up in the demands of my classes and forgot about it.

•

29. Those three stories are "The Blank," "A Slow Death," and "Extermination."

And then I did get a call. It came a little after six in the morning. I was still sleeping after a long night of studying and writing. I stumbled my way to the phone, figuring it was probably an emergency. "Hello?" I managed.

"Brian Evenson?" a man's voice said, pronouncing it like the word "even" rather than with a short *e*.

"Evenson," I said, correcting him, still not sure what was going on, "yes, that's me."

"This is Gordon Lish."

Figuring it was a friend messing with me, I almost hung up. If I'd been more awake, I probably would have.

•

I talked to Lish for perhaps ten minutes. During that time, he told me that Ashbel Green had passed along *Siege*—which, Lish said, was not a novel, not something he could publish as a book, but there was still something there, something original. I had potential, he said, and he could bring that potential out, could make me one of the best writers of my generation, just as he had done for Barry Hannah, Mary Robison, Amy Hempel, and Raymond Carver. But I should move to New York. I should abandon everything and come to New York to take his writing class.

Um, I said. I'm in graduate school. And when that didn't seem to be enough to convince him I shouldn't move immediately, I mentioned that I was also married. And that I was expecting my first child. That last fact made him immediately stop talking about me moving to New York (he would never suggest it again), and made the conversation slightly more relaxed.

There was something in *Siege*, he told me, something there, some wonderful moments but they needed to be extracted from the whole, allowed to breathe. No, he couldn't publish *Siege*, not in its current form—to do so wouldn't do me any favors. But did I know his magazine *The Quarterly*?

I did, I told him, and mentioned Darrell Spencer and several stories by others I'd read in the early issues, and the fact that some of my classmates had sent them to him. Strange, he said, how many good writers seemed to come out of Utah, from the Mormons. What was the reason for it? Did I know?

I said I didn't.

So, I was to do what I could with the material in *Siege* and send it his way to look at, and other stories, as well. Or perhaps he would mark it up and show me how to do it. And then we would see. All right?

All right, I said.

There was probably more but that's what I remember. I remember as well somewhere in the conversation him realizing that there was a three-hour time difference since I was in Seattle and he was in New York and that he was calling me at six in the morning, but he didn't apologize for this, only commented on it as a fact. I remember too that periodically he would stop me from talking and address someone in the room with him. And I remember how abruptly he hung up.

I crawled back into bed.

"What was that about?" asked my wife, half asleep.

"I'm not sure," I said. I closed my eyes, but quickly realized there was no way I'd be able to get back to sleep. I was too busy imagining myself as one of the best writers of my generation.

·

I've always been grateful to Ashbel Green, who made the choice to pass my "novel" along when he didn't have to. That I had come to Lish's attention at all was luck.

I've found since that more than a few writers have stories like that, something random happening that led to them being noticed or published. The paths that lead to becoming a published writer are discontinuous and not predictable. When I told the story of how I met Lish to writer François Camoin, he told me how his own first book of fiction had been published because he'd accidentally left a copy of the manuscript at a vacation house he'd rented and the next person to stay at the house was an agent who discovered it, read it, took him on as a client and found him a publisher.

There are also a great many talented writers who never get those lucky breaks.

I was tremendously flattered by Lish's call. Hard not to be when you're a young developing writer with just a few magazine credits to your name and suddenly you have an editor from a New York publishing house encouraging you, even an editor you didn't send directly to. And the person who had edited Carver no less, a writer who had been very important to you. And he clearly thought a lot of you if he thought you could be one of the best writers of your generation.

Later, when I began to meet other writers who Lish was publishing at Knopf or in *The Quarterly*, I realized I wasn't unique.

"Did he give you the speech?" was among the first things one of them said to me.

"The speech?"

"You know, how if you come to New York and take his class he can make you into one of the best writers of your generation?"

As it turned out, Lish had said what he said to me to a great many people.

•

Lish and I had several years of back and forth on the stories that would become part of *Altmann's Tongue*. Most he would not take; I sent him dozens of stories from late 1990 or early 1991 until *The Quarterly* shut down in 1995. He published thirteen stories in all, most of them quite short. When he didn't take a story he would often send the story back with a row of x's where he stopped reading, with the suggestion that that was where I had gone wrong. Often, when he did like a story he would send me back a copy with fairly substantive revisions in his own hand—not just corrections here and there, but sometimes large bits of the story cut or changed. Such edits made the story swifter, more minimal, moving forward by nuance and implication.

Was I comfortable with such revisions? Sometimes yes, sometimes no. It made me remember my BYU class-mate trying to justify to himself publishing a Lish-revised story that he wasn't completely comfortable with. Often, I liked Lish's revisions, and felt they brought out things that had been submerged in my stories that I wanted brought out. Lish made me think very consciously about the language of the stories, made me feel that every word mattered, made me a more language-conscious writer. Often, even if I felt comfortable with the revision and sent Lish back a version of the story that incorporated them, perhaps along with a few more revisions of my own, he might still send an additional edit back, and might still not accept the story for publication.

At other times, I felt like Lish's revisions could hijack a story. The first time that happened, I called Lish on the tele-phone and told him I wasn't inclined to make the revisions and he said Fine, he was busy, and hung up. The next four or five stories I sent he returned to me rejected and with-out comment and I thought that might be the end of my time publishing at *The Quarterly*, and that I was never going to have a book contract with Knopf. But I kept submitting, meanwhile publishing stories in other magazines. Eventually Lish and I discovered we shared an interest in philosophy, and perhaps as well by dint of practice my writing improved. In any case, he ended up being more responsive.

I mention all this to try to give at least some sense of what it was like to work with Lish, and what it must have been like for Carver. Lish was—still is—incredibly charismatic. He'd thought a lot about language and about fiction, had very firm ideas about it, but also had wider taste than he was generally given credit for. I knew he liked minimalism, but it was Lish who introduced me as well to Cormac McCarthy, to Joy Williams, to Thomas Bernhard. I watched him once do an incredibly smart close reading of an exuberant McCarthy passage and then on the same day speak compellingly and convincingly of the seemingly unadorned beginning of a Leon Rooke story. He tended to provoke, but if you took a different path than he suggested and achieved strong results he would be full of nothing but praise. If you tried and failed, however, he might berate you. Above all, he always suggested, what was important was the work and the success of the work.

Still, Lish's personality was large enough and his aesthetic sufficiently developed that it was a balancing act as a young writer not to allow yourself to be absorbed by it, particularly when he was suggesting dramatic cuts. The several years I spent sending work to *The Quarterly* were years in which I was building an aesthetic of my own, refining my style partly with the help of and partly in opposition to

Lish. I made some false steps, as all writers probably do, and there's one story in *The Quarterly* that I've never collected. But the pressure of that interaction also led to "Altmann's Tongue," which was the first story I wrote where I really felt like I had developed my own distinctive style and concerns, and then to "The Father, Unblinking" and "Stung," which deepened those concerns. But, I saw as well, if you weren't careful it would be very easy to end up with a story that was, aesthetically speaking, a good story, but one that you didn't feel connected to. If that were to happen, it would, no doubt, be a disorienting experience, even a disheartening one, particularly if you were praised for that story much more than for other stories you felt more connected to.

Again, I thought of Carver.

•

I hadn't met Lish. I knew him only through letters and phone calls. I was living on the opposite side of the country from him and had neither the money nor the time to travel to New York to meet him. By the time my daughter Valerie was born in 1991, I'd been given a teaching assistantship at University of Washington.[30] Connie had finished at BYU by correspondence and was enrolled in the

---

30. Another stroke of luck—a professor I had had for a class and who was on the committee to give out TAs came to By George café on the day they were being distributed, realized with surprise I was working at a café instead of teaching, and decided I deserved a TA.

MA program in the French department and was teaching as well. Even so, we were poor enough that we were going to the food bank on a regular basis. When our ailing car broke down, the Bishop of the local Mormon church felt sorry for us and sold us a rusted out old Suburban with 300,000 miles on it for $50—that would be our only car until I got an NEA fellowship in 1995 and used it to buy a slightly used minivan.

At the end of 1992 I was close enough to finishing my PhD that I decided to go on the job market. I was writing my thesis, *The Carnival of Negativity*, which was a critique of Mikhail Bakhtin that used late eighteenth- and twentieth-century novels to suggest a tradition of carnival that was different from the positive, grotesque celebration that Bakhtin's *Rabelais and His World* suggested. Perhaps not surprisingly, only two schools wanted to interview me, one of which was Brigham Young University.

I'd vowed, once I left Utah, never to go back, but now, with a young daughter and my wife pregnant with another child, I began to feel that any job would do. So, just after Christmas, I flew out to the MLA convention, which was being held in New York.

My BYU interview seemed to go well—I was, after all, being interviewed by former teachers. My other interview, with Valdosta State College in Georgia did not. An hour before my interview, when I was eating in a deli, my brief-case was stolen. It had little of value in it, but it did have the information about where the Valdosta State interview was to be held. Since this was in the days before email was readily accessible, I had to go to insane lengths by phone to track down the room number. By the time I managed to figure it out, I was twenty minutes late to the interview and spent a good chunk of the time I did have apologizing.

When Lish found out I was going to be in New York between Christmas and New Year's, he invited me to his apartment—he had to stay home because of his wife Barbara, who had Lou Gehrig's disease and who would pass away from complications related to that illness a year and a half later. That evening, after both interviews were over, I took the subway to the Upper East Side and met Lish for the first time. He offered me a drink, but I was Mormon at the time and didn't drink. He offered me snacks, I no longer remember what, but remember eating something. He did not eat, but kept urging me to eat. Lish talked about DeLillo and his work. He mentioned that DeLillo's novel *White Noise* had been originally called *Panasonic* but DeLillo had had to change the name after he made the mistake of asking Panasonic for permission and they denied it. We talked about movies, which he knew a lot about: I could (just barely) keep up because of working in an independent movie theater in Seattle. He talked about his son who was getting involved in martial arts and who either had dropped out of Harvard or was about to drop out. He told me that Harold Brodkey had contracted AIDS (Brodkey would die in 1996 of complications related to the illness), then went on to praise Brodkey's stories and to talk about an 1100-page manuscript of a novel of Brodkey's called *Party of Animals* that he thought was the best thing Brodkey had ever done, but that Brodkey had changed it to *The Runaway Soul* and, in the process, had made it a lesser work. When I sat in on one of his week-long intensive classes in San Francisco, he'd tell the same story about Brodkey's novel, the language almost verbatim.

I don't remember what else we talked about, but we talked for four or five hours. Throughout he was urbane, charismatic and performative, but also kind and solicitous. Near the end, he asked how my interviews had gone, and when I told him he said, "You told them of course that you have a book of stories coming out with Knopf?"

No, I admitted, I hadn't.

"Tell them," he said. "You'll have a contract once the offices reopen after the new year."

That was how I found out that Knopf was going to publish my first book.

Six

I DON'T KNOW WHO FIRST MENTIONED TO ME THAT LISH had sold his archives to the Lilly Library. It might have been one of the other writers who worked with Lish and published in *The Quarterly*. Or it might have been Lish himself, in passing. In any case, as soon as I found out, I was intrigued. I was a scholar as well as a fiction writer, and I was above all intrigued to see how Lish had edited those American writers who had influenced me: Raymond Carver, Amy Hempel, Don DeLillo, Barry Hannah, and David Ohle, to name a few.

Whoever it was, as soon as I found out, while still a graduate student at University of Washington, I wrote to the Lilly Library, letting them know I'd be interested in coming to look at Lish's papers and would be in the area in October. On October 2, 1991, I had a reply from the Lilly Librarian saying that the materials weren't unpacked and it would be several months before they'd be ready to view.

So, I'd have to wait. I got distracted by other things—finishing my dissertation, writing *Altmann's Tongue*, having children—and so it wasn't until I was settled as faculty member at BYU in 1995 (I'd gotten the job that I interviewed for in late 1992, but delayed coming until January of 1994) that I took steps to go to the Lilly Library.

I wrote again at that time and found that the Lish archives were still in the process of being sorted, but the Carver materials were among the things that had been sorted. I applied for a Lilly Library Helm Fellowship and received it. I borrowed a university-owned early laptop, a strange bulky thing that weighed about twenty pounds and came in a specially padded case, and was given careful instructions on how to park the drive whenever I moved it. On July 20th, 1995, I flew to Bloomington, Indiana.

The next day, at 9 a.m., I was at the Lilly Library when it opened. I introduced myself to the librarians in the reading room, learned the rules. By 9:30, I had opened my first box.

•

By the time I'd finished my week at the Lilly Library I had typed seventy-one single-spaced pages of notes on Carver's letters to Lish, largely consisting of descriptions and partial transcriptions of the letters the two exchanged.

I had thirty-eight single-spaced pages documenting Lish's revisions of Carver's stories, detailing the most important things that Lish had omitted from or added to the stories. I also came away with fourteen pages of notes on Lish's revisions of other writers (none quite so extensive as Carver, but many quite extensive nonetheless—and of course not everything had been sorted when I visited in 1995), as well as fourteen pages about the letters from others that Lish had received.

Because of copyright considerations, I won't quote what I saw, or even describe it in much detail except in instances where that information is already available through other published sources. There were letters from Carver and other writers, some of which were quoted in D. T. Max's August 9, 1998 *New York Times Magazine* article "The Carver Chronicles", the piece which is largely credited with exposing to the general public Lish's intensive editing of Carver.[31] The Max article also reproduces part of a marked-up manuscript page of "Fat" with Lish's edits and marks on it. But the first published reproduction of a Carver manuscript page occurred three years earlier, in Carol Polsgrove's 1995 history of *Esquire*

---

31. D.T. Max, "The Carver Chronicles," *The New York Times Magazine* 8/9/1998, 34-40, 51, 56-57. In fact, it was known, among scholars at least, well before that. Indeed, Kirk Nesset reported in 1994 that Tess Gallagher had admitted there had been "severe editing by Gordon Lish." Cf. Kirk Nesset, *The Stories of Raymond Carver* (Athens, OH: Ohio University Press, 1994), 310. Other brief mentions and rumors abound, going all the way back to the 1980s.

magazine, *It Wasn't Pretty, Folks, But Didn't We Have Fun?* which reproduces the fifth page of the manuscript for "Neighbors" with Lish's extensive revisions.[32] Indeed, Polsgrove was the first critic to write substantively about the extent of Lish's editing of Carver, and has never been properly credited for this. Speaking of "Neighbors" she says, "On several pages of the twelve-page manuscript, fewer than half of Carver's words were left standing. Close to half were cut on several other pages... Uncut, Carver's manuscript read a good deal more like an ordinary, realistically rendered story . . ." (241) She goes on to suggest that the intention of the revision (and indeed, by implication of the creation of minimalism) was to give the story "a flat ironic style characteristic of a writer he particularly liked, James Purdy."[33]

I came to Purdy's work well after I came to Carver's, but I liked his work a great deal, well enough to correspond with him for a decade, and think him currently as a massively underrated writer. Like Polsgrove, I agree that Lish must have admired Purdy's economy of style, his precise control of language in the stories of *Color of Darkness* and

32. Carole Polsgrove, *It Wasn't Pretty, Folks, but Didn't We Have Fun?*: *Esquire in the Sixties* (New York: W. W. Norton, 1995). The manuscript page reproduction is on page 242, with discussion of Carver's editing of Lish on the pages directly before and after.

33. Lish mentions Purdy as who he had in mind "more than anyone else" (206) in his interview with Christian Lorentzen published in *The Paris Review*.

Children Is All, and his ability to conclude stories without the dramatic finality of most of his contemporaries. Purdy's stories as well often revolve around the collapse of communication within families, a collapse which applies as well to Carver's *Will You Please* and *What We Talk About.*

William L. Stull and Maureen P. Carroll's notes at the back of the Library of America's *Raymond Carver: Collected Stories* also provide ample quotation of materials in the archives, as well as long quotations of correspondence between Lish and Carver—the most important of these is a letter on pages 992–96 in which Carver expresses his doubts and fears about Lish's severe revision of the manuscript that would become *What We Talk About When We Talk About Love.* Carol Sklenicka's excellent biography similarly draws upon archival materials found in the Lilly Library and elsewhere. I do not quote below anything that hasn't already been publicly cited in a widely-distributed format.

Though I'll also say that there are things that haven't been discussed publicly in the Lish archives that are incredibly interesting, and aggressive editing of writers from Barry Hannah[34] forward that are deserving of serious scholarly consideration.

•

34. For an example of how Lish edited Hannah, see the revised manuscript page from Hannah's *Ray,* reproduced at the beginning of Lish's *Paris Review* interview, page 194.

I started with Carver's manuscripts, thinking that it would make sense to look at them in some detail before beginning to examine the correspondence surrounding them. I made notes as I went. Here's an example of my notes about what is probably the most extreme case among the stories I came across (though there were others that weren't that far from it):

> **Mr. Fixit: was "Where is Everyone?" Would become "Mr. Coffee and Mr. Fixit."**
> **Bookdraft 1: Mostly follows the published version.**
> **15 pages.**
> Page 1: maybe four lines cut.
> 2: 55% gone. Much deleted having to do with the lover, his being shot, his time in jail.
> 3: 50% gone
> 4: 22 lines deleted, 2 lines written in by Lish.
> 5: 25 of 27 lines deleted
> 6: ~22 lines deleted.
> 7: 25 of 27 lines deleted
> 8: 26 of 27 lines deleted. Two lines written in by Lish.
> 9: 26 of 27 lines deleted.
> 10: 18/27 lines deleted.
> 11: 21/27 lines deleted.
> 12: All but 2 lines deleted. Several lines written in by Lish.
> 13: 26/27 lines deleted.

14: 26/27 lines deleted.

15: 17/17 lines deleted.

Bookdraft 2:

Title Mr Fixit: Written in: "Mr Coffee &"

1: 30%

2: reworded quite a bit.

3: 25%

4: 3-4 lines rewritten, 2 lines del., 20%

5: the last three lines in the published version are written in verbatim by Lish.

[This seems, as far as I can tell, identical to the published draft.]

In other words, Lish took Carver's fifteen-page typescript manuscript, cut and edited it by hand until, when retyped, it was five pages. Then he edited it still further until in the end it was cut by 78 percent from its original length.[35] That was the version that appeared in *What We Talk About When We Talk About Love*.

Now that *Beginners*, the draft manuscript that would become *What We Talk About When We Talk About Love*, has been published, it's easy for anyone to get a feel for how much Lish changed the stories, without visiting the Lish archives. Had Carver published *Beginners* without the drastic cuts by Lish that made it *What We Talk About*, the

35. 78 percent is the estimate that Stull and Carroll give in their notes to *Raymond Carver: Collected Stories*.

book would have been double its length, closer in length to *Cathedral*, though the quality of the stories would not have been nearly as strong. Indeed, *Beginners* is closer in feel and quality to *Furious Seasons* than to *Cathedral*. In addition, Lish made critical changes to the endings. My sense, having read both *Beginners* and *What We Talk About When We Talk About Love* next to each other, is that there is little doubt that had *Beginners* been published untouched by Lish it would not have attracted the attention it did.[36] Indeed, those elements of *What We Talk About* which struck reviewers as new and innovative result largely from Lish's revisions.

That Carver could "restore" some of his stories in his new and selected collection *Where I'm Calling From* without meeting much resistance on the part of his audience seems to me less an indication that the Lish-edited versions in *What We Talk About* were worse than, first, a sign that Carver had created a new audience with *Cathedral*, one that was oriented toward less radical notions of narrative, and, second, an indication of a backlash toward minimalism.

Of the nine stories from *What We Talk About* that Carver chooses to include in *Where I'm Calling From*, four appeared first in *Furious Seasons* and are restored, to a great

36. Indeed, the very non-scientific study allowed by comparing the number of Amazon.com reviews each book received suggests that *What We Talk About* is still by far the most read of the two, garnering 180 reviews as opposed to *Beginners'* six reviews. Though perhaps people who prefer *Beginners* aren't the kind of people likely to post a review on Amazon.com.

degree, either to the form in which they appeared in that book, or to what he revised them to be in *Fires*. Of the other stories he includes, he takes one of the ones Lish revised least ("The Calm," cut by 25 percent according to Stull and Carroll) and then three that are revised on the lower end of the scale—"Why Don't You Dance?" (cut by 9 percent, though there's some suspicion there is a revision missing), "A Serious Talk" (cut by 29 percent), and "Gazebo" (cut by 44 percent). In fact, "What We Talk About When We Talk About Love" (50 percent) is the only story from the eponymous collection that Carver chooses to include as is that is revised over 45 percent by Lish.

These choices suggest that Carver wanted to shift the image of *What We Talk About When We Talk About Love*, that he was very uncomfortable with Lish's revision. Curiously, however, Carver does not revise the stories in *Where I'm Calling From* which are taken from *Will You Please Be Quiet, Please*, even in the case of a story like "Neighbors, which we have clear evidence that Lish dramatically revised.

•

To give you a better sense of how severely Lish revised *Beginners* to make it *What We Talk About When We Talk About Love*, it probably makes sense to start by simply listing the percentages that Stull and Carroll give for how much each story was revised. But before I do, I want to be clear about the context.

I was a writer myself. I was looking at revisions of stories by a writer I genuinely admired and who had been quite influential on my own development as a writer. I had been revised by Lish and had both accepted and rejected those revisions at different times. I had heard other young writers talk about how Lish had revised them, so had some sense of how aggressive an editor he could be, and that he might be more aggressive with some writers than others. I had already compared some of the Carver stories that existed in more than one published version, so even had a sense of the extent of the revisions.

However, even in that context, the revisions were more extensive than I had imagined. Looking at them felt, in some respects, like a violation. I felt like I was seeing something that, ethically speaking, I wasn't sure I should see. Something I wasn't sure I *wanted* to see. It's one thing to say that "Where Is Everyone?" lost eleven of its fifteen pages when it became "Mr. Coffee and Mr. Fixit." It's quite another to look at those pages and see the proliferation of scrawled marks in Lish's hand—to see, for instance, that of the last four pages of "Where Is Everyone?" everything but a line or two per page has been crossed out, with Lish writing in as much as he preserves. It's quite another to see how Lish has crossed out the last five pages of the nineteen-page original version of "Tell the Women We're Going" and written in the abrupt ending that you love so well. It makes you feel, well, weird, and if you're a writer it makes you think, too, about every edit you've accepted or rejected, makes you wonder how those edits change you, not only as a writer but as a person. Do they damage you? Do they diminish you?

•

All books, of course, go through multiple drafts, most of them with an editor. Some of those editors are aggressive, others not. Some would be if they weren't so overworked. Ideally, an editor is there to help further the author's intentions and to make the author's book function as effectively as possible. Readers generally see only the finished draft, the published book, and rarely have a sense of all the steps that it took to get there.

In that sense, Carver went through something that every writer goes through, albeit quite a bit more aggressively than most. At the same time, being a story writer, Carver had published his stories first in magazines, and Lish was revising them later for the collection, so early readers, particularly friends and admirers of Carver, often knew both versions. They were able to see that in moving from magazine publication to book publication the stories hadn't only gotten shorter, they often seemed to have acquired a different worldview. A bleaker, harsher view of humanity. Considering that Carver had stopped drinking, was happy, and was with a woman he loved, Tess Gallagher, one would have expected the stories to move in the opposite direction.

That's not to say that happy writers can't write bleak work. Indeed, I'm probably the test case for that—I often write exceptionally bleak work, but am a generally quite happy person who looks, roughly, like a cross between Santa Claus and Robin Williams. But, as the letter Carver wrote to Lish protesting the changes suggests, he was not that sort of writer. Those changes in worldview are entirely due to Lish's edits.

Many of Lish's edits are consistent with what other editors might try to do to improve a writer's work and make it more effective for readers. But there's a strain in Lish's editing that goes beyond this, that hijacks the aesthetic and worldview of the story, that pushes the story along a different vector. As I say, I like the Lish revisions better—they were influential on me, because of the specifics of my own worldview and my own reading of a certain absurdist strain of European literature, in a way that *Beginners* would not have been. But I can like the stories while still having reservations about the way that Lish made Carver's stories do something different than what Carver was comfortable with. Similarly, I can admire *Chinatown* as a movie while still having reservations about the way Roman Polanski manipulated Faye Dunaway to get her jittery (and quite effective) performance. But, if I'm to be honest, every time I watch that movie I have to think about and sort through that manipulation and my feelings about it again. Just as, now that I know as much as I do about Lish's editing of Carver, it's hard for me not to have to sort through it again every time I read a Carver story.

In that aspect of his editing of *What We Talk About*, Lish strikes me as being somewhat like that old friend who wants you to still be the brash, reckless person you were when you were younger. His editing of Carver's worldview in *What We Talk About* makes it more like *Will You Please*'s worldview, but even more severe. It's as if, seeing Carver's trajectory toward a fuller more developed story, Lish wants to make it do just the opposite. Are the results good stories? Yes. Are they stories that Carver can live with? Maybe. But not comfortably.

•

Seeing the Carver manuscripts at the Lilly Library was a little like being backstage at a magic show and seeing how the trick is done. As someone who had worked with Lish, I already had peeked through the curtain, but I'd never seen a writer's entire career laid out in front of me like this, his manuscripts crossed out and marked up. It makes me think of the movie version of *The Wizard of Oz*, when they discover that the giant image of the great and powerful Oz is being made by a very different individual pulling controls behind a curtain. When he realizes he's discovered, the man shouts, through his projected voice, *Pay no attention to that man behind the curtain!* But how can you not, once you see clearly that a man is there?

•

Here are Lish's cuts: [37]

"Why Don't You Dance"	cut by 9%
"Viewfinder"	cut by 30%
"Where Is Everyone?"/	
"Mr. Coffee and Mr. Fixit"	cut by 78%
"Gazebo"	cut by 44%
"Want to See Something?"/	
"I Could See the Smallest Things"	cut by 56%
"The Fling"/"Sacks"	cut by 61%
"A Small Good Thing"/"The Bath"	cut by 78%
"Tell the Women We're Going"	cut by 55%
"If It Please You"/"After the Denim"	cut by 63%
"So Much Water So Close to Home"	cut by 70%
"Dummy"/	
"The Third Thing That Killed My Father Off"	cut by 40%
"Pie"/"A Serious Talk"	cut by 29%
"The Calm"	cut by 25%
"Mine"/"Popular Mechanics"	cut by 1%
"Distance"/"Everything Stuck to Him"	cut by 45%
"Beginners"/	
"What We Talk About When We Talk . . ."	cut by 50%
"One More Thing"	cut by 37%

•

37. These figures are derived from William Stull and Maureen Carroll's assessments in the notes of *Raymond Carver: Collected Stories*.

How far can you cut a story before it stops being the story it was and becomes something else? I can lose 22 percent of myself and still survive, as I know from my time in the hospital in 2011. I might be able to lose 30 percent, even 40 percent, but rapidly I'd reach a point of diminishing returns. After that, I might still be alive, but the only way to have me lose more would be to amputate a limb. If I was to go on a starvation diet and then amputate all my limbs, could I lose 78 percent of my body weight? Probably not. Even if I could, I'm not certain what was left would be me.

It's probably not coincidental that, after having thought seriously about Lish's severe editing of Carver, I went on to write a novel, *Last Days*, about an amputation cult.

Carver went from having a series of stories he could recognize himself in to stories that he couldn't. It must have been, on some level, horrifying.

At the same time, I'll continue to insist that yes, whether you see Carver or Lish as more responsible for these stories, they are excellent stories. American literature would be less without them.

•

The changes Lish makes are radical. For instance, here's the ending of "One More Thing" as it was published in *The North American Review*—more or less the same as the ending that Carver uses in *Beginners*:

"I just want to say one more thing, Maxine. Listen to me. Remember this," he said. "I love you. I love you no matter what happens. I love you too, Bea. I love you both." He stood there at the door and felt his lips begin to tingle as he looked at them for what, he believed, might be the last time. "Goodbye," he said.

"You call this love, L.D.?" Maxine said. She let go of Bea's hand. She made a fist. Then she shook her head and jammed her hands into her coat pockets. She stared at him and then dropped her eyes to something on the floor near his shoes.

It came to him with a shock that he would remember this night and her like this. He was terrified to think that in the years ahead she might come to resemble a woman he couldn't place, a mute figure in a long coat, standing in the middle of a lighted room with lowered eyes.

"Maxine!" he cried. "Maxine!"

"Is that what love is, L.D.?" she said, fixing her eyes on him. Her eyes were terrible and deep, and he held them as long as he could.[38]

And here's the ending as it appeared in *What We Talk About*:

38. "One More Thing," *North American Review* 3.3 (Spring 1981): 28–29.

"I just want to say one more thing," he said.

But then he could not think what it could possibly be. (159)

The *What We Talk About* version opts for a less dramatic ending, the emotions and sentiment not breaking through as they do in the earlier version. Where the first version offers one final attempt at communication and understanding, at least going through the motions, Lish ends even before the attempt. Though the Lish-edited ending might go too far in its restraint, Carver's certainly did not go far enough.

•

Lish's internal revisions of the stories often involved removing the context from the stories' events. The feel of the stories changed in revision, Lish working to rid them of their hopeful moments, of anything to give the sense that the characters still have functional connections with one another, and of any move toward transcendence, redemption or consolation.

This is made clear in the ending of "Tell the Women We're Going." When Carver published the story a decade earlier as "Friendship" in *Sou'Wester* in 1971, there were a great many details included concerning Jerry's pursuit of the girl he will eventually kill. The narrative follows her, for instance, as she hides herself in a cave and waits as she hears Jerry come down the path. He throws pieces of shale back at her to get her to come out, and when she does and tries to escape, he blocks her way and begins to fondle her. She pushes him off balance and runs past. He pursues her, pins her down, and after a struggle rapes her. Nervous that she'll tell, he starts hitting her, then hits her with a rock, then crushes her head with a bigger rock. The many details elided in "Tell the Women We're Going" are provided in "Friendship," and they there are in the *Beginners* version as well.

Shortly after, Bill, nervous, rushes up to see both Jerry and the dead girl, Jerry holding his bloody rock. In "Friendship" things end as follows:

> Bill felt himself shrinking, becoming thin and weightless, at the same time he had the sensation of standing against a heavy wind that was cuffing his ears. He wanted to break loose and run, run, but someone was moving towards him. He waited for a moment longer, then put out his hand as the tears began to course down his cheeks. As if the distance now separating them were nothing, he took the other's arm. [39]

In other words, Carver allows Jerry and Bill to have a moment of reconciliation over the corpse of the girl one of

39. "Friendship," *Sou'wester Literary Quarterly* (Summer 1971): 61–74.

them has murdered. Such a reconciliation seems staged to me, too consciously literary, and also profoundly false. In the collection, "Tell the Women We're Going" ends long before, giving no real sense of the pursuit and no sense (as discussed earlier) that a murder is coming until the last few words of the story.

One would expect that Carver, in the interim between the publication of "Friendship" and its revised publication as "Tell the Women We're Going" in 1981 in *What We Talk About*, might have trimmed the story as a whole down and brought the story's ending closer to the later version. In fact, the version that Carver gave Lish for the collection has moments that are expanded rather than trimmed. The last paragraph of the story is about twice as long as the conclusion of "Friendship" quoted above:

> Bill felt himself shrinking, becoming thin and weightless. At the same time he had the sensation of standing against a heavy wind that was cuffing his ears. He wanted to break loose and run, run, but something was moving towards him. The shadows of the rocks as the shape came across them seemed to move with the shape and under it. The ground seemed to have shifted in the odd-angled light. He thought unreasonably of the two bicycles waiting at the bottom of the hill near the car, as though taking one away would change all this, make the girl stop happening to him in the moment he had topped

the hill. But Jerry was standing now in front of him, slung loosely in his clothes as though the bones had gone out of him. Bill felt the awful closeness of their two bodies, less than an arm's length between. Then the head came down on Bill's shoulder. He raised his hand, and as if the distance now separating them deserved at least this, he began to pat, to stroke the other, while his own tears broke. (*Collected Stories*, 843–44)

At least instead of the distance between Jerry and Bill closing, the distance is acknowledged in this version, but this ending is almost excruciatingly articulated, and Carver seems to me to be striving too hard to make the scene "mean" something. Lish was absolutely ruthless with such moments.

The power of the ending as revised by Lish resides in its shock. It comes down like a hammer upon the reader, its last words gathering a remarkable sense of power, throwing the reading into shock and yet leaving the exact circumstances of the murder open to the imagination. The imagination is always more effective at filling in gaps like this than anything that words attempt to pin down on the page. Carver's "Friendship" ending, with the embrace, seems an odd attempt to bring Jerry back into the human circle. The remnants of that are still visible in the story as Carver revised it for *Beginners*. Lish's ending remains strong for me precisely because of its coldness, its refusal to humanize either Jerry or the situation: that strikes me, paradoxically, as the more ethical choice. Indeed, it can be read as a judgment against Carver's initial sentiment. While Carver allows Jerry to begin to be drawn back into the human circle, albeit temporarily, Lish permits no such gestures of kinship.

·

I could compare the versions of most of the stories found in *Beginners* and *What We Talk About When We Talk About Love* and show similar things, moments where the editorial choices are, in my opinion, quite good, but where they seem to go against Carver's original intent. But this book is not a comparative study of *Beginners* and *What We Talk About Love*—although I'm surprised that no Carver scholar has yet written such a book. Such a book would not only tell us a lot about Carver and the way his stories developed; it would also tell us a lot about editing and editors, and would raise a host of thorny ethical dilemmas.

Publicly, Carver was often shifty about Lish's editing of his work. Think again of how careful he was to avoid admitting Lish's role in editing *What We Talk About* when he wrote the afterword for *Fires*. Even when he is talking about a story that Lish cut by 70 percent ("So Much Water So Close to Home"), he doesn't mention Lish. He says not "Lish rewrote these stories," but "I like to mess around with these stories." The closest he comes is saying, of "Distance" and "So Much Water," that "They had both been largely rewritten for the Knopf book." He can't quite bring himself to claim that he rewrote them, but he doesn't admit Lish did either. He keeps the language passive—as if he's just talking about himself liking to mess around with his stories—implying that he was the one doing the rewriting.

Both D. T. Max's "The Carver Chronicles" and the notes found in *Raymond Carver: Collected Stories* quotes from a July 8, 1980, letter that Carver wrote to Lish, saying he didn't want to publish *What We Talk About* as Lish had edited. Wrote Carver, "Maybe if I were alone, by myself, and no one had ever seen these stories, maybe then, knowing that your versions are better than some of the ones I sent, maybe I could get into this and go with it." Max's read of this is that Carver feared getting caught—and this, indeed, is supported by other portions of the same letter. "How can I explain to these fellows when I see them, as I will see them, what happened?" Lish's response? To move forward with the revisions essentially unchanged. Said Lish to Max, "My sense of it was that there was a letter and that I just went ahead." (40)

Shame is a terrible thing, and often leads people to act strangely. Carver did not feel connected to the stories in *What We Talk About* after having published them. He did not want to move forward, and would have pulled out if he'd been allowed, if Lish hadn't talked him out of it. So the book that really helped make Carver's reputation also potentially made Carver feel like an imposter.

But when he published *Cathedral* Carver stood up for himself, keeping Lish from heavily editing the stories, keeping the worldview of the stories essentially the same. What Carver called the "fullness" and "generosity" of the stories was a result of Lish's editorial hand being largely stayed. That book received critical acclaim—even more so than *What We Talk About*. I don't like that book as well as *What We Talk About*, but I do applaud Carver for publishing the book he wanted to publish, in the form he wanted to publish it in.

Where Lish's editing is problematic are the moments when, instead of bringing out elements already inherent in a Carver story, he took the story in a new direction, gave the story a new sensibility and ethos that was more his own than Carver's. Lish could be seen as experimenting behind the scenes at Carver's expense, though it was Carver who received both the praise and the blame.

•

Lish's revisions of the stories in *What We Talk About When We Talk About Love* challenged Carver's self-confidence. Often they cost him a great deal personally, even as they gave him critical recognition. It is undeniable that Lish took liberties with Carver. Lish put Carver in the awkward position of having to defend publicly work which Carver himself was not always certain he stood behind. Though one must not forget that at any stage in the process Carver could have simply refused had it been important enough to him. Though the changes were made by Lish, Carver chose, both implicitly and explicitly, to accept them.

•

In any case, one cannot claim that Lish is the author of Carver's work. Leslie Field, speaking of Thomas Wolfe's editors, says something applicable:

> . . . one may legitimately ask, "Did they overstep the bounds of acceptable editorial practice?" Perhaps this question can never be answered satisfactorily. Evaluations of editing fall within the provenance of judgment. What may be too much editing for me may be insufficient for another. But Perkins, Nowell, and Aswell were editors, not writers. Wolfe was responsible for the original creations. Without him the editors had nothing to shape.[40]

The same can be said of Lish. Though he was able to shape Carver's material in a way that Carver could not (and in some cases did not want to) shape it, he was still working with material Carver had given him.

While Carver remains one of the foremost figures of

40. Leslie Field, *Thomas Wolfe and His Editors* (Norman, OK: University of Oklahoma Press, 1987), 179–80.

American short fiction, one of the few contemporary writers with a volume in the Library of America, Lish's career after Carver slowly declined. He was fired by Knopf in 1995 and no other publishing house would hire him. *The Quarterly* folded after thirty-one issues. Lish's own work, despite the clear strengths of certain of his novels and stories, has never had a fraction of the acclaim that Carver's has had. Now, at eighty-three, with a reputation for being a brilliant but difficult renegade, he teaches private fiction writing workshops.

Maxwell Perkins, in a letter to Ernest Hemingway about Thomas Wolfe, pinpoints the dilemma of being an aggressive editor. When Wolfe asks if he will take responsibility for the editing, he says, "I will be blamed either way."

Or in Lish's words, "I've been decried for a heinous act. Was it that? Me, I think I made something enduring. For its being durable, and, in many instances, beautiful."[41]

41. Lish, "Editing," 207.

Seven

I CAME BACK FROM THE LILLY LIBRARY WITH MY HEAD
spinning. Indeed, it was spinning even before I left. I'd been
arriving as soon as the library opened at nine and working until it closed at six, sometimes taking thirty minutes
for lunch but other times working straight through. There
was so much material to look at and I had so little time.
The second day I was there, it was a Saturday, which meant
the library closed at 1:00, and on Sunday it wasn't open at
all, so I had a day and a half early in my stay where I was at
loose ends. I spent it at the main library on campus, which
was open Sundays. I was allowed in but unable to check
out books, so I went and found a copy of all of Carver's
books and Barry Hannah's *Ray*, thinking that it would be
good to refamiliarize myself with them and have in mind
the finished products as I continued to look over the manuscripts. I read mostly in the part of the library that housed
Tibetan books, partly because I was less likely to be bothered there, partly because after poring over manuscripts and

letters there was something comforting about being surrounded by oddly cased scroll-like books written in a language I couldn't even begin to decipher.

Tired of fighting Mormon controversy over my first book and realizing that if I wanted to publish another book I was best off doing it from another university, I left Brigham Young University shortly after I arrived home from the Lilly, taking an unpaid leave and accepting a one-year position at Oklahoma State University. I was busy enough with the move and with getting re-established that I put my Carver notes aside for a time. Soon, this one-year position converted to a tenure-track one, and I cut my ties with Brigham Young University for good. It took me longer to sort through my relationship with Mormonism and leave the church, but eventually I would manage to do that as well.

By early 1996, I'd come to work on my Carver material again, and had begun to write an essay about the way Lish had edited Carver. I'd been in touch with James Plath, who was involved in putting together a collection of critical essays on Carver.[42] I'd written to him about what I'd found in the Lilly Library, and he'd expressed interest in considering my essay.

As I drafted the essay, I found that I continued to have a hard time deciding what I thought exactly. I still liked

---

42. I don't think such a collection ended up being published at the time, though Plath did edit in 2013 *Critical Insights: Raymond Carver* with Salem Press.

Carver's stories but seeing the materials in the Lilly Library had made my enjoyment of them more . . . complicated. It was very hard for me to read a story from *What We Talk About* without part of my head noting where the changes had been, what the story had been before Lish revised it. Plus, Lish had been the editor of my first book. He no longer was my editor, but we still communicated, and talked a lot about philosophy in particular, about our mutual admiration for thinkers like Alphonso Lingis and Giorgio Agamben. That also complicated my feelings for the situation. I didn't want to attack someone who had been important to my own career, but at the same time I didn't want to bend over backward to avoid saying things that needed to be said. I also was worried about equating Carver's situation too much with my own, somewhat different one. I told myself I wanted to be as honest as possible. But I was not sure what that meant exactly.

I took several runs at it. Finally, near the end of Oklahoma State's academic year I had something I thought I could show to Plath. I sent it off to him, along, I believe, with a letter in which I asked if Gallagher had any of the Lish letters, thinking it would be useful to see that side of the conversation, and asking too how difficult it might be to get permission to quote from Carver's letters and manuscripts.

On June 3rd, I had a fax back from him telling me that, according to Bill Stull, Gallagher didn't have any of the Lish letters, and that those letters perhaps no longer existed. He addressed the issue of permission to reprint excerpts from the letters. I would need to get permission from Gallagher, but again Stull, he said, had told him it wouldn't be a problem. His suggestion was to search for permissions only after bringing the essay close to the final form.

I started working on revisions of my Carver essay. In the meantime, my British agent, Giles Gordon, asked if he could see a copy. We'd spoken about the essay and Giles, who had been both an editor and author before becoming an agent, was curious. I faxed him a copy.

Giles read the essay and extolled it to a few people, perhaps partly testing the waters for possible publication of it in a non-academic venue. He might have even shared a draft of it with some—since Giles died from complications after a fall in 2003, at this point I have no way of confirming this. I don't believe I asked him to do this, and probably would have asked him to stop had I known.

Among the people who learned of the article was a writer who was a friend of Carver's. Apparently, he informed Gallagher of it. Suddenly, I discovered my article was no longer under consideration.

On July 28, 1996, I wrote to Gallagher, offering her the opportunity to review my article—less of a draft at this point, but still developing. I heard nothing for several months until, on September 11, Gallagher's copyright attorney wrote to me, misspelling my name, to advise me that they would be strict when it came to determining whether there was infringement of copyright of the unpublished letters and manuscripts. I wrote back on September 19th after consulting someone at Oklahoma State who specialized in copyright law, saying that I was convinced that my usage fell "under notions of scholarly use," mentioned that I had offered Gallagher a chance to review my article in July, and indicating that I would be willing to show them passages which might be open to debate. "Then, if you have objections to particular instances, we might be able to resolve them before the article's publication."

On September 27, I had a letter back from Gallagher's lawyer, indicating they had been given a draft of my proposed article by a third party and declaring that in their opinion I had excessively used unpublished work. They mentioned a draft being distributed through my agent in the UK, as well as through Gallagher's "publishing associates" (by which I assumed, correctly or incorrectly, that she meant the people assembling the volume of critical essays on Carver). The draft I had shown to Giles was an early draft. It was, indeed, a draft that contained material that would have demanded permission from Gallagher, but I had known that and had raised that very question with James Plath. He had been told by Stull that permission would not be a problem, but that we should wait to request it until the essay was close to its finished form. Gallagher's attorney went on to suggest that copies of Carver's unpublished manuscripts seemed to have been improperly copied, retained and distributed and should have been returned to Carver, that nobody should ever have been able to see them.

I wrote back once more, hoping in part to correct misconceptions, saying:

> From what you say of my proposed article on Raymond Carver, it is clear that we are not discussing the same version of the article: your unnamed third party has given you a much earlier draft. The current version does not quote from Carver's correspondence. In addition, in many cases it chooses to quote from published earlier versions of the stories rather than the unpublished manuscripts. You should note as well that it is my understand that my British agent never actively distributed the proposed article for publication, though I was aware that he had shown it privately to several people . . .

> I chose to show the earlier version of the article to a limited number of people, and to these only because a third party involved in Carver studies led me to believe that Ms. Gallagher's permission to quote from Carver's unpublished letters and manuscripts could be readily obtained by him and his associate on my behalf. When it became undeniably clear to me that he was mistaken, I stopped showing that version of the article to others.

> I currently have no intention of abandoning my proposed article on Carver, though at present I have no

fixed plans for the article's publication... I also have no intention of publishing material which would infringe on Ms. Gallagher's copyright, while recognizing there is room for interpretation of what those rights protect ...

I don't believe I received a reply. If I did, I have not preserved it, which would be unlike me. I continued to work on my Carver paper, cutting out anything that might be open to legal challenge, removing all quotations from Carver's letters, but I found myself less and less interested in the project. I didn't need to publish the paper—at BYU I had been hired as an academic, but now that I was at Oklahoma State I was hired as a fiction writer. Indeed, I was the only fiction writer on faculty, which, considering we had a PhD in creative writing, meant I was swamped. So I would track down another early published version of a Carver story, work on the article, then get caught up in other things and put it aside.

I still had the notion I might publish the article when, sometime in 1997, I was contacted by Dan Max. He'd heard, he said, that I'd done some work on Carver and that I'd looked at the Lish archives in the Lilly Library. He was thinking about pitching a story on Lish's editing of Carver but wanted my opinion: was what was there worth looking at?

Absolutely, I said. But you're likely to run into permissions trouble with Carver's widow.

I began to give him a sense of what was in the archive, and then stopped. "Look," I said, "go take a look for yourself. I promise you it's worthwhile."

Soon Max had gone to the Lilly Library and had pitched the article to the *New York Times Magazine*. The files were more thoroughly sorted than when I'd been there, and he found things that I hadn't found. Early on, Max wanted to make sure he wasn't stepping on my toes by pursuing the article, but since my article planned to be more scholarly than exposé, I didn't feel that he was. In any case, it was better, I felt, for the information to be out in the open rather than to be floating around as innuendo and rumor. For it to be published at all made me feel less like I was the caretaker of the information. It was a relief. And when the article did come out I was also happy to have it acknowledged in print that, "Carver's widow and literary executor, the poet Tess Gallagher, effectively blocked [Evenson] with copyright cautions and pressure." (Max, 34-35) I believed then, and still believe, that the attempt to protect Carver's reputation by controlling information about how his stories were conceived did not do Carver any favors.

When Max's article came out, it ran not only a facsimile of Lish's edits of Carver's story "Fat," but quoted from Carver's unpublished letters to Lish.

I was surprised Gallagher had allowed that.

When I shared my surprise with a friend, "It's the *New York Times*," he said. "The story was going forward with or without a lawsuit. She knew that."

•

In the end, my experience trying to write an article on Lish and Carver all feels a little like a Carver story to me. Or, rather, a Carver story as revised by Lish. There's little communication, a lot of missed chances, a lot of frustration, and no happiness at the end. If my agent hadn't shared the essay with the wrong person, the article might well have come out and the Carver-Lish story would have been productively discussed by scholars before becoming a focus of literary controversy. If I'd been allowed to have a conversation with Gallagher rather than her barricading herself behind lawyers, perhaps things would have been different. If, if, if. And so on. At the time it all happened, more than twenty years ago, it made me angry, and frustrated me.

At the same time, even back then I couldn't help but sympathize both with Carver and with his widow's desire to maintain his reputation. Two years before, after complaints by anonymous letter to upper Mormon church leaders about my first book, *Altmann's Tongue*, I'd had to leave BYU. This was at least in part because Lish had, in writing the jacket copy for *Altmann's Tongue*, identified me as "a devout Mormon, an unequivocal believer, a bishop in the Church . . . a faculty member at Brigham Young University." Indeed, the anonymous letter that had started everything in motion, that I was forced to respond to, had indicated that it was because I was actively identifying myself as a member of the Mormon church that I couldn't be allowed to continue teaching at BYU. I'd had reservations about that jacket copy as well, and had raised them with Lish. I'd pointed out that it was inaccurate to say I was a bishop since I never was—I was a counselor in a bishopric which was somewhat different. I also objected to not seeing it sooner. But I had waited too long to question this and the books were already in production. Because of that, I could at least imagine how, after sending Lish a long letter telling him not to proceed, in Stull and Carroll's words in the notes to the *Collected Stories*: "Not long afterward, Carver spoke to Lish by telephone. No record of their conversation is preserved, but Lish's point of view prevailed." (996)

Now I see it more as everybody doing their best but being too blinkered and too much at cross purposes to be able to agree, too wounded or anxious to see past their first impressions. It begins with Carver acting like the alcoholic he was and hiding the fact of Lish's extensive editing even from people quite close to him. Or maybe it begins with Lish being more concerned to have the fiction be as good as he felt it could be than he was with the wishes or impulses of his friend. It continues with Carver not being able to bring himself to read Lish's first revision of *What We Talk About When We Talk About Love* and then reading Lish's second revision and being stunned by what Lish had done to his stories and writing him to ask him to stop production of the book. It continues when "Lish's point of view prevailed." It continues with Gallagher trying to minimize or control talk about Lish editing Carver, then with me trying to write an article while not being sure exactly where my allegiances should lie, then with Giles Gordon's no doubt well-meaning attempt to share my article, then with a friend of Carver's well-meaning attempt to let his widow know that someone was going to break the story and break it in the wrong way, then with various letters from lawyers, Dan Max's wide release of the Carver story, and finally here we are today, some of us dead, some still alive, with certain people still feeling so anxious about the relationship of Carver to Lish that they can't pay attention to the quality of the stories themselves.

•

This was the chapter of the book I was most reluctant to write, partly because I find it exhausting to revisit all this, partly because it seems like so much effort was wasted in trying to hide (and, later, in trying to bring out) the fact that Carver was heavily edited by Lish, partly because in the end I would like to feel it is the strength of the stories themselves that matter. Says Carol Polsgrove, "If you exalt the individual writer as the romantic figure who brings out these things from the depths of his soul . . . then, yes, the awareness of Lish's role diminishes Carver's work somewhat. But if you look at writing and publishing as a social act, which I think it is, the stories are the stories that they are."[43]

43. Quoted in Max, 51.

•

Strangely enough, I'm finishing the first draft of this chapter on the day that Caladex arrived at my house to gather the thirty-eight boxes that constitute my literary archive and ship them off to the Beinecke library. Everything that I've been carting around—all the various drafts and partial drafts of my essays on Carver, the letters from Gallagher's copyright attorneys, six folders of letters from Lish, written correspondence and emails to and from Dan Max, James Plath, Giles Gordon and countless others concerning Carver, manuscripts of my stories that Lish published, manuscripts of my stories and novels written after Lish was no longer my editor, so many other things that touch on every aspect of my life as a writer, my life as a human—no longer belongs to me.

I'm surprised how good this feels.

When you have an abrupt break, when someone or something that was in your life is suddenly gone, your relationship to the past changes. When you give up drinking, as Carver did, it dramatically reorders the world around you. When you nearly die in the hospital and go through a breakup, it does the same. It's easy to look back on your past and think "That isn't me." When people expect you to act like you did before, you might want to get away from those people—as, indeed, Carver wanted to get away from Lish. He was ready, as a writer, to be someone else, but Lish wanted him to be even more intensely the writer that he had already made him.

Guess who won?

Nobody.

Afterword

BACK IN THE 1997, ANOTHER WRITER, FROM NEW YORK, also published by Lish, listened very attentively as I told him that I had visited the archives, told him what was there, and told of how I had been cautioned by Gallagher's lawyer. Then he said, "You know what the problem is? Nobody is asking whether Carver is a good writer. He's not. None of those books are any good."

It shocked me at the time, still does a little. Even though I remember the disappointment of my first experience rereading Carver. I reread *What We Talk About When We Talk About Love* just a month or two after I read it the first time, hoping to have the same, almost revelatory experience I'd already had. But I didn't have it. I wasn't as impressed. I could see how the stories were put together, could see how they achieved their effects. I would describe this to people when I talked to them about it as "being able to see the stories' bones." That's an experience I never have with Isak Dinesen or Henry James—I can reread a story of theirs closely after a first reading and it remains just as powerful, just as strong, just as mysterious. Indeed, for many years I chose not to re-read *What We Talk About When We Talk About Love* for fear of seeing even more of the bones. I would read individual stories, mainly because I would teach them, but until this year it had been several decades since I had reread a full Carver book.

But rereading now, after many years, my age even older than what Carver's was when he wrote them, myself even older than Carver was when he died, the stories work for me again. I found myself finishing the last story in the collection and everything coming together, the entire shape of it shimmering there, an aesthetic object, for just a moment, in a way that made me not only understand again why I loved Carver so much when I was learning to write, but made me feel it.

I've explained what it is I like about *What We Talk About When We Talk About Love*, and told you enough about myself that you can, perhaps, understand why. I liked the book when I first encountered it back when I was eighteen. I continued to like it, albeit in a more complicated way, even after I understood some of the complexities and challenges of its composition. I tried to not like it when I was threatened with legal action by Carver's widow, and for many years after read it only in bits and pieces. But having just returned to it, I still think it's an excellent book. I think American literature would be weaker without it. I would, certainly, be a weaker writer without it. It is a book that matters.

I can't insist you agree with me, and I wouldn't want to, but I'll say it again. I like this book. It is a book that matters. Despite all the complexities of its editing, many of us would be lesser writers without it.